The French Economy in the Twentieth Century

This new textbook examines the spectacular transformation that the French economy has undergone over the past century. Jean-Pierre Dormois offers a general introduction to the major trends as well as recent transformations of French society, and an overview of modern economic development. He tackles the key themes associated with the French 'path of economic development' – Malthusianism, exceptionalism and Colbertism. Other chapters address standard economic issues relating to the role of human capital formation, economic institutions and openness to the rest of the world. The author examines and interprets trends and features of the period as a whole, and sets them in a wider European framework. This book offers students a helpful and concise summary of recent research, and presents a uniquely synthetic view of the French economy in the twentieth century. It will have broad appeal for students and teachers of French and of European history and economics.

JEAN-PIERRE DORMOIS, a former Knox Fellow at Trinity College, Cambridge, is currently Professor of Economic History at the Université Marc-Bloch in Strasbourg. Among his books are *L'Economie française face à la concurrence britannique* (Paris 1997), and he has edited *The British Industrial Decline* (London 1998).

New Studies in Economic and Social History

Edited for the Economic History Society by
Maurice Kirby
Lancaster University

This series, specially commissioned by the Economic History Society, provides a guide to the current interpretations of the key themes of economic and social history in which advances have recently been made or in which there has been significant debate.

In recent times economic and social history has been one of the most flourishing areas of historical study. This has mirrored the increasing relevance of the economic and social sciences both in a student's choice of career and in forming a society at large more aware of the importance of these issues in their everyday lives. Moreover specialist interests in business, agricultural and welfare history, for example, have themselves burgeoned and there has been an increased interest in the economic development of the wider world. Stimulating as these scholarly developments have been for the specialist, the rapid advance of the subject and the quantity of new publications make it difficult for the reader to gain an overview of particular topics, let alone the whole field.

New Studies in Economic and Social History is intended for students and their teachers. It is designed to introduce them to fresh topics and to enable them to keep abreast of recent writing and debates. All the books in the series are written by a recognised authority in the subject, and the arguments and issues are set out in a critical but unpartisan fashion. The aim of the series is to survey the current state of scholarship, rather than to provide a set of pre-packaged conclusions.

The series has been edited since its inception in 1968 by Professors M. W. Flinn, T. C. Smout and L. A. Clarkson, and is currently edited by Professor Maurice Kirby. From 1968 it was published by Macmillan as *Studies in Economic History*, and after 1974 as *Studies in Economic and Social History*. From 1995 *New Studies in Economic and Social History* is being published on behalf of the Economic History Society by Cambridge University Press. This new series includes some of the titles previously published by Macmillan as well as new titles, and reflects the ongoing development throughout the world of this rich seam of history.

For a full list of titles in print, please see the end of the book.

The French Economy in the Twentieth Century

Prepared for the Economic History Society by

Jean-Pierre Dormois
Université Marc-Bloch, Strasbourg, France

PUBLISHED BY THE PRESS SYNDICATE OF THE UNIVERSITY OF CAMBRIDGE
The Pitt Building, Trumpington Street, Cambridge, United Kingdom

CAMBRIDGE UNIVERSITY PRESS
The Edinburgh Building, Cambridge, CB2 2RU, UK
40 West 20th Street, New York, NY 10011-4211, USA
477 Williamstown Road, Port Melbourne, VIC 3207, Australia
Ruiz de Alarcón 13, 28014 Madrid, Spain
Dock House, The Waterfront, Cape Town 8001, South Africa

http://www.cambridge.org

© The Economic History Society, 2004

This book is in copyright. Subject to statutory exception
and to the provisions of relevant collective licensing agreements,
no reproduction of any part may take place without
the written permission of Cambridge University Press.

First published 2004

Printed in the United Kingdom at the University Press, Cambridge

Typeface Plantin 10.5/12 pt.   *System* LATEX 2$_\varepsilon$ [TB]

A catalogue record for this book is available from the British Library

Library of Congress Cataloguing in Publication data
Dormois, Jean-Pierre.
The French economy in the twentieth century / prepared for the Economic History
Society by Jean-Pierre Dormois.
    p.   cm. – (New studies in economic and social history ; v. 49)
Includes bibliographical references (p. 141) and index.
ISBN 0 521 66092 0 – ISBN 0 521 66787 9 (pb.)
1. France – Economic conditions – 20th century – Textbooks.   I. Title: French
economy in the 20th century.   II. Economic History Society.   III. Title.
IV. New studies in economic and social history ; 49.
HC276.D673   2004
330.944′08 – dc22   2003065425

ISBN 0 521 66092 0 hardback
ISBN 0 521 66787 9 paperback

Contents

List of figures	*page* vi
List of tables	vii
Preface	xi
List of acronyms	xiv
1 The end of French exceptionalism?	1
2 French economic performance in international perspective	11
3 France and the wider world	27
4 The changing face of Colbertism	43
5 The institutions of French capitalism	63
6 Labour: the French at work	82
7 Plough and pasture: lifeblood or drain?	101
8 Industrialisation, de-industrialisation, postindustrialisation	112
Conclusion	128
Glossary	132
A national portrait gallery of twentieth-century France	134
Bibliography	141
Index	146

Figures

2.1 The French inflation record, 1920–90	page 20
2.2 French unemployed as a percentage of the working population, 1950–2000 (ILO definition)	25
3.1 Rate of nominal protection of French imports, 1900–2000	30
4.1 Share of public spending and the public debt in GDP, 1900–2000	49
5.1 Education attainment levels by age cohort 1901–96	72
6.1 Total numbers of the working population, 1901–96	84
6.2 Wind of change after the 1945 election (cartoon)	86
6.3 The fall in the working hours per year and the rise in pay, 1901–95	90
6.4 Measures of labour force quality and human capital stock, 1901–95	94
6.5 French unemployment rate across a century	98
7.1 French foreign trade in cereals, 1913–45	105
8.1 Distribution of new equity inflows compared with existing assets, mid-1950s	118

Tables

1.1 Age structure of French and British population, 1914	page 2
1.2 Population growth per annum by periods, 1870–1998	3
1.3 Distribution of immigrants by continent of origin, 1946–90	5
1.4 Distribution of workforce by sector, 1906–1998	8
1.5 Age distribution of French population	9
2.1 Average annual growth rate of GNP in the twentieth century	12
2.2 Productivity measured by GNP per employee per year	14
2.3 Average annual growth rate of GNP among OECD countries, 1950–2000	18
2.4 The achievement of the 'Trente Glorieuses'	21
3.1 Degree of openness (proportion of exports in GNP)	28
3.2 Simple linear regression impact of French trade openness on economic growth	31
3.3 Share of world manufactured exports, 1913–98	33
3.4 Share of French trade with present EU member countries	41
3.5 Outstanding moves in comparative advantage, 1967–97	42

viii List of tables

4.1 Size of the civil service and its share in total employment	45
4.2 Public expenditure as a proportion of GDP	47
4.3 Devaluations of the franc, 1928–58	54
4.4 Stop-and-go, French style: expansionary cycles (trough to trough)	60
5.1 Distribution of French firms by corporate status, 1969	67
5.2 Distribution of credit by main depositors, 1990	70
5.3 Domestic expenditure on R&D, its sources and performance indicators, mid-1990s	74
5.4 Some notable French inventions and discoveries, 1890–1984	76
5.5 'Representative' labour union federations and their representativeness	78
6.1 Distribution of female employment by broad categories, 1938 and 1985	89
6.2 Average number of annual working hours and weeks of paid holiday, 1913–90	92
6.3 Distribution of primary and disposable income between 1970 and 1997	93
6.4 Productivity bonus by level of education, France–USA, 1977	96
6.5 Unemployment rates by sex and age categories, 1986	99
7.1 The effects of urban migration on labour productivity, 1896–1999	103
7.2 Distribution of farms according to size, 1955–98	107
7.3 Total output by main crops, 1970–2000	109
7.4 CAP 'direct aid' subsidies by crop in 1999	110
8.1 French labour productivity compared to British, 1906/7 and 1930/1	114
8.2 Distribution of French firms by size of payroll, 1906–66	115
8.3 Sectoral and economy-wide annual growth rates, 1905–75	116

8.4 Changes in manufacturing employment by sectors,
    1960–2000   119
8.5 Foreign trade in manufactures, 1974–2000   120
8.6 Sectoral and economy-wide labour productivity
    1901–38   121
8.7 Employment, value added and labour productivity
    across the economy, 2000   126

Preface

The aim of this book is to present a comprehensive and synthetic view of the French economy in the twentieth century. It was intended as a sequel to Colin Heywood's volume on the nineteenth. Writing it at the beginning of the new millennium has entailed both advantages and drawbacks. Most historical accounts currently available stop short of the developments of the last twenty years (or alternatively treat them piecemeal), which means that they have yet to receive the full scrutiny they deserve. By contrast, this study attempts to provide an examination and interpretation of trends and features of the most recent period and integrate them in the longer term as well as set them in a wider European framework. Most historical surveys break down the twentieth century into several sequences or episodes (prewar, wartime, interwar, postwar), or they treat economic trends of the Third Republic (1870–1940), the Vichy regime (1940–44), the Fourth Republic (1944–58) and the Fifth Republic (since 1958) separately. This segmentation has been reinforced by the unrelenting specialisation of historical scholarship.

Rather than resorting to the chronological subdivisions imposed by political developments, the option adopted here has been to tackle broad (and popular) themes recurrent in the literature on French modern economic development. I begin with the classic claim, endemic among native (and sometimes foreign) authors, of a French *Sonderweg*[1] or exceptionalism. There persist to this day more and less extensive versions of this particular belief, ranging from an assertion of the primacy of geographical and cultural

---

[1] A term used by the German historical school to stress the supposed uniqueness of German history in the modern period.

factors in a nation's path of development to the implicit contention that the commonly recognised 'laws of economics' do not apply to France. In this respect, the twentieth-century record points decisively towards an alignment of French practice and behaviour (if not always attitudes or representations) on a common Western pattern, a phenomenon sometimes referred to as 'Americanisation'. The examination of French economic performance in Chapter 2, when set in a European framework, further weakens the case for uniqueness. One of the powerful levers for such 'regional convergence' is to be found in the switch, with regard to trade and investment, from isolation to growing interdependence among Western countries between the first and the second halves of the twentieth century: this provides the guiding thread of Chapter 3. Outsiders and insiders alike often associate the French 'model' of development with an extensive and skilful form of statism (Chapter 4). Cost–benefit analysis of government intervention, initiative, and influence in the market has not been carried out systematically, but the patchy record suggests that the French brand of interventionism has been less successful and more akin to that found elsewhere in the world than was previously thought. Other collective institutions outside – but sometimes subject to – the state, and essential to the operation of a market economy, such as firms, banks and schools, are reviewed in Chapter 5. The contention that French workers were intrinsically partial to leisure is scrutinised in Chapter 6, which supplies the salient details of the composition of, and changes in, the labour force and human capital formation. Chapter 7 recounts the vicissitudes of France's agriculture which, despite its apparent capacity to fuel a positive trade balance and maintain the natural beauty of the countryside, illustrates how collective representations, skilful bargaining and good intentions can help create an economic nonsense. Finally, Chapter 8 documents the build-up of domestic industry and the subsequent transition from an industrial to a service economy which the country has undergone in the course of less than three generations. On the basis of the most recent information a few clues are offered in the Conclusion as to where the French economy may be heading at the turn of the twenty-first century.

The literature on the present subject is, as one would imagine, enormous. The bibliography at the end of the volume has been compiled with a view to providing, besides the sources tapped by the author, a list of the most prominent works on the subject. Unfortunately, a lot of the research carried out by economists and historians in the postwar period was done in the spirit of the times, i.e. with a conviction of the incluctable progress of socialism. 'The fall of the Berlin wall [1989] has caught many of them on the wrong side of it' (Flandreau) so that either the material needs to be re-examined in a new light or the conclusions drawn from it must be reformulated. In this respect, comparative economic history, it is hoped, constitutes the safest bulwark against the temptation to view the outside world, past and present, through the eyes of one's own fantasies.

I am very grateful to Michael Sanderson and Maurice Kirby, editors of the series, for commissioning and supporting this project and I owe a special debt to Elizabeth Howard for her patience and special attention in guiding my steps towards the completion of the manuscript. In researching for this volume I had to appeal to a number of librarians who have helped reduce my ignorance of the subject. My thanks go first and foremost to the staff at the Montpellier INSEE information section and the librarians of the economics faculty there. I have belatedly realised that regular reading of *The Economist* magazine had powerfully helped me to write economic English sufficiently well to be understood by native speakers. The *tour de force* which this book represents for me is a personal tribute to the quality, informative as well as literary, of its contents. This homage, however, is not meant to exonerate the author from his blunders, errors, omissions and misinterpretations, which remain his own.

Acronyms

AAL	Autorisation Administrative de Licenciement (official permission for dismissal – 1975–86)
ADP	Aéroports de Paris
AFP	Agence France Presse
ANACT	Agence Nationale pour l'Amélioration des Conditions de Travail
ANPE	Agence Nationale pour l'Emploi (job placement agency, created 1967)
APA	Allocation Personnalisée d'Autonomie (old-age allowance for the disabled elderly, est. 1998)
ART	Agence de Régulation de Télécommunications (Telecom regulator)
ASSEDIC	Association pour l'Emploi dans l'Industrie et le Commerce (1959)
BFCE	Banque Française du Commerce Extérieur
BIT/ILO	Bureau International du Travail (International Labour Office)
BNCI	Banque Nationale du Commerce et de l'Industrie
CAP	Common Agriculture Policy (created 1962)
CCF	Crédit Commercial de France
CDC	Caisse des Dépôts et Consignations (est. 1816)
CDD	contrat à durée déterminée (short-term, typically eighteen-month work contract)
CDF	Charbonnages de France (state-owned collieries)
CDI	contrat à durée indéterminée (long-term work contract)
CEA	Centre à l'Energie Atomique
CECA/ECSC	European Coal and Steel Community

List of acronyms xv

CED/EDC	(failed) European Defence Community, 1952–54
CEE	French acronym for European Economic Community (EEC, est. 1957)
CEEA/EURATOM	Communauté Européenne de l'Energie Atomique
CFDT	Confédération Française Démocratique du Travail (Social Democratic Labour Union; split off from FO in 1964)
CFP	Compagnie Française des Pétroles (est. 1924)
CFTC	Confédération Française des Travailleurs Chrétiens (Christian Democratic Labour Union)
CGC	Confédération Générale des Cadres (managers' union)
CGE	Compagnie Générale d'Electricité
CGP	Commissariat Général au Plan (planning agency, est. 1945)
CGPF	Confédération Générale de la Production Française (1919)
CGPME	Confédération Générale des PME, q.v.
CGT	Confédération Générale du Travail (oldest trade union federation, est. 1895)
CMU	Couverture Médicale Universelle (free medical care for the needy; est. 1997)
CNEP	Comptoir National d'Escompte de Paris
CNES	Centre National des Etudes Spatiales (space agency)
CNJA	Centre National des Jeunes Agriculteurs (young farmers' union, rival of FNSEA, q.v.)
CNPF	Confédération Nationale du Patronat Français (successor to CGPF q.v.; est. 1946, employers' federation)
CNR	Conseil National de la Résistance (unified by Jean Moulin in 1943)
CNRS	Centre National de la Recherche Scientifique (est. 1945)
COB	Commission des Opérations de Bourses (French securities exchange commission, est. 1967)
COFACE	Compagnie Française d'Assurance pour le Commerce Extérieur
CSG	Contribution Sociale Généralisée (1990)
CUMA	Coopérative d'Utilisation du Matériel Agricole

DATAR	Délégation à l'Aménagement du Territoire (town and country planning agency, est. 1963)
DGE	Direction Générale à l'Equipement (est. 1941)
DGT	Direction Générale des Télécommunications (est. 1944)
DOM	Département d'outre-mer (overseas department)
ECB	European Central Bank
ECU	European Currency Unit (introduced 1979) forerunner of the Euro
EDF	Electricité de France (electricity utility)
EEC/EU	European Economic Community (1958), European Union (since 1992)
ENA	Ecole Nationale d'Administration (est. 1945)
ENS	Ecole Normale Supérieure (est. 1794)
ERAP	Entreprise de Recherche et d'Activités Pétrolières
ERP	European Recovery Program (Marshall Plan 1948–52)
FDES	Fonds de Développement Economique et Social (est. 1948 succeeded FME, q.v.)
FDI	foreign direct investment
FEOGA	Fonds Européen d'Orientation et de Garantie Agricole (EEC organisation managing farming aid, est. 1962)
FME	Fonds de Modernisation Economique (1947)
FNSEA	Fédération Nationale des Syndicats d'Exploitants Agricoles (mainstream farmers' union)
FO	Force Ouvrière (non-Communist, split off from CGT, q.v., 1947)
FORMA	Fonds d'Orientation et de Régulation des Marchés Agricoles (est. 1960)
FSGT	Fonds Spécial de Grands Travaux
GATT	General Agreement on Tariffs and Trade (1948–93)
GDF	Gaz de France (gas utility, est. 1945)
GEN	Grandes Entreprises Nationales (major public corporations or SOEs, q.v.)
GIE	Groupement d'intérêt économique (1967)
GPRF	Provisional government of the French Republic (1944–6)
HEC	Hautes Etudes Commerciales, France's first business school (est. 1881)

List of acronyms xvii

HLM	Habitations à Loyer Modéré (council housing)
HSP	Haute Société Protestante (refers to influential Protestant banking families during the Third Republic)
IAA	industries agroalimentaires (food industries)
INRA	Institut National de la Recherche Agronomique
INSEE	Institut National des Statistiques et des Etudes Economiques (statistical agency, est. 1945)
ISF	impot de solidarité sur la fortune (wealth tax)
IT	information technology
IUT	Institut Universitaire de Technologie (similar to polytechnics; created 1966)
IVD	Indemnité Viagère de Départ (retirement allowance for ageing farmers)
LoN	League of Nations (1920–45); forerunner of United Nations (est. 1944)
MEDEF	National Employers' Association, successor to CNPF, q.v. (1992)
OECD	Organisation for Economic Co-operation and Development (succeeded OECE 1960)
OECE	organised 1948 to apportion US aid under the Marshall Plan (1948–52)
ONIB, ONIC	Office National Interprofessionnel du Blé [des Céréales] (wheat/cereals marketing board)
ORTF	Office de Radiodiffusion Télévision Française (public broadcaster)
OS	ouvrier spécialisé (unskilled operative)
PCF	Parti Communiste Français (est. 1920)
PME	petites et moyennes entreprises (small and medium-sized firms)
PS	Parti Socialiste (est. 1971; successor to SFIO, q.v.)
RATP	Régie Autonome des Transports Parisiens
RDS	Remboursement de la dette sociale (additional payroll tax, created 1995)
RMI	Revenu minimum d'insertion (1990)
SA	société anonyme (joint-stock company)
SAFER	Société d'Aménagement Foncier et d'Etablissement Rural
SARL	société anonyme à responsabilité limitée (limited liability company)
SEEF	Service des Etudes Economiques et Financières (Central economic intelligence bureau at the Ministry of Finance)

xviii List of acronyms

SEM	Société d'Economie Mixte (mixed company)
SFIO	Section Française de l'Internationale, Ouvrière (Second International, Amsterdam 1889)
SMIG	Salaire Minimum Interprofessionnel Garanti (minimum wage, est. 1950; became SMIC in 1970)
SNC	société en nom collectif (partnership)
SNCF	Société Nationale des Chemins de Fer Français (state-owned rail operator, est. 1937)
SNCM	Société Nationale des Compagnies Maritimes (state-owned shipping company)
SNIAS	Société Nationale des Industries Aéronautiques et Spatiales
SOE	state-owned enterprise
UAP	Union des Assurances de Paris (insurance conglomerate)
TOM	territoire d'outre-mer (overseas territory)
TUC	Travaux d'Utilité Collective (1985)
TVA	Taxe sur la Valeur Ajoutée (VAT, est. 1954)
UDCA	Union de Défense des Commerçants et Artisans (1953)
UEP/WPU	Western Payment Union (1948)
UNEDIC	Union Nationale pour l'Emploi dans l'Industrie et le Commerce (1959)
WPU	see UEP
WTO	World Trade Organisation (succeeded GATT in 1993)

Chapter 1
The end of French exceptionalism?

> The French distinguish themselves by thinking they are universal.
> Paul Valéry (1871–1945)

In early January 2002, Jean-Marie Messier, head of the water-distribution-to-mobile-phones conglomerate Vivendi Universal, announced in a resounding interview the end of *l'exception française*. The furore which then arose from virtually every corner of politics and the media revealed the deep-rooted belief that France had remained, and should remain for the foreseeable future, a society different from its neighbours and partners. Different parties attach different meanings to this claim but all amount to a call to the government to set standards for society at large and enforce them. What Messier may have been voicing, however, was not so much a normative judgement as a statement of fact, pointing out the relentless erosion of cultural identities in the Western world and beyond. In this he was undoubtedly right. This process of convergence and standardisation, often referred to as 'Americanisation', in many aspects of social life, economic and otherwise, has affected France as it has its European neighbours, with increasing vigour in the second half of the century.

1. The end of Malthusianism

Convergence has affected first and foremost French patterns of demographic behaviour. The first Western nation historically to have undergone a demographic transition (a drastic reduction of its birth rate), France saw its population virtually stagnate for close to a hundred years from the middle of the nineteenth century

Table 1.1 Age structure of French and British population, 1914

%	France	Britain
aged below 20	33.6	40.1
aged 20–60	53.6	51.4
aged 60 and over	12.8	8.5

onwards. In 1936 it numbered thirty-nine million people, barely more than in 1836 (thirty-six million). 'Malthusian' behaviour (the voluntary limitation of family size) has been linked to precocious and widespread birth-control practices,[1] conceived as a strategy to maintain property holdings intact since the Code Civil (1804) stipulated the equal division of the family estate between siblings. As a result, the single-child family was especially prevalent in France before the Second World War.

From a demographic standpoint, the twentieth century can be conveniently divided into three successive and distinct periods: until 1945; from 1945 to 1968; and from 1968 onwards. Up to the Second World War the prolonged stagnation of the French population had far-reaching implications. In terms of numbers France was no longer a 'heavy-weight' on the Continent as other countries caught up with her; this affected the relative size of her army and therefore her military potential). But it meant also that France's population was ageing much faster than that of other comparable countries (see Table 1.1). The falling birth rate sometimes prevented the replacement of generations: from 1908 to 1912 and again between 1935 and 1939 France experienced negative population growth. Both before and after the First World War, foreign immigrants – first, Italian and Belgian, and later Polish and Spanish – came to fill the consequent gap in the workforce. France's ailing population was further hit by the hecatomb of the world wars. In the first, of all belligerents (bar Serbia) France suffered the highest casualty rate relative to its population. In addition to its 1.4 million dead, a vast majority of them young men, the number of wounded

---

[1] A British historian quipped that nineteenth-century French demographic behaviour amounted to 'copulation without population'.

Table 1.2 Population growth per annum by periods, 1870–1998

Period	France	Western Europe
1870–13	0.18	0.77
1913–50	0.02	0.42
1950–73	0.96	0.70
1973–98	0.48	0.32

(2.5 million) and the birth deficit in wartime (1.7 million) caused a gender imbalance in the interwar years which further depressed the birth rate. France paid a less catastrophic toll in the Second World War: less than half the number of lives lost in the first war and merely 400,000 births forgone (as a result of the internment of 1.8 million prisoners of war). But, unlike after the former war, the consequences of the latter were soon erased by the 'baby boom' which swept Western Europe in the aftermath of the Second World War.

No explanation can fully account for the reversal of the fertility rate which occurred in 1942, in the darkest hours of Nazi occupation, but the pickup proved to be lasting: in the thirty years which followed, France experienced, on the strength of a fertility rate of over 2.5 children per woman, the fastest rate of natural increase in its recent history (this was paralleled in terms of economic growth). After the Second World War the French population increased by a third, to fifty-two million by 1971. Having been outpaced until the mid-century by most European countries, France found itself leading the pack (see Table 1.2). The immediate causes of this change are fairly well documented: they can be safely traced to a sharp fall in the death rate, especially the infant mortality rate (which fell twenty fold in the course of one generation) and the consequent extension of average life expectancy. At the beginning of the century, this was 48.5 years for men and 52.4 for women; it is today 75 and 82 respectively.

But such developments also obviously involved deep cultural, even psychological, features which were common to most advanced countries at the time. In the French case the 'baby boom' can be seen as a conjunction of two phenomena: on the one hand the maintenance, in the context of sharply falling infant mortality, of relatively high fertility; on the other, the standardisation of sexual and family behaviour. Whereas before, population increases could be ascribed to the contribution of large families (while 20 per cent of women remained childless), from the 1950s onwards the vast majority of married couples conceived and raised between two and three children: the 'nuclear' family became the dominant pattern as the marrying age significantly decreased and divorce remained marginal (10 per cent of all marriages).

All this changed again in the wake of the 'sexual liberation' of the 1970s. In 1969, for the first time in a generation, the fertility rate fell below 2.1 (the minimum to ensure the replacement of generations). Marriage became disconnected from sex and procreation and families became more 'uncertain' as well as more brittle. The age at marriage (and procreation) was progressively delayed to the late twenties–early thirties. Today 40 per cent of all marriages end in divorce; 28 per cent of children are born out of wedlock; and around 220,000 abortions (legalised by the 'loi Veil' in 1975; fully covered by social security since 1981) are carried out each year.

Alone among all European countries France 'exported' very few of its children to the 'new worlds' in the nineteenth century (barely half a million left its shores permanently between 1820 and 1914). Conversely, because of its weak demography the country had to 'import' foreign workers, starting at the time of the Great Depression (1873–96) later in that century. This made France a forerunner in European settlement patterns since all Western countries now have sizeable foreign communities on their soil. Furthermore, the integration of these 'guest workers' was made relatively easy by liberal nationality legislation (law of 11 August 1927).

For most of the twentieth century, it was principally Europeans from neighbouring countries who moved to the labour-starved industrial conurbations of the north and east. Prior to the First World War, cross-border workers from Belgium in the north and Spain and Italy in the south accounted for a fair number of the transfers (France's Italian-born community was second in size only to that of the USA). In the 1920s, Poles first and later Spaniards joined them – the latter mostly Spanish republicans. At the height of immigration to France in 1931, three million foreign workers and their families had settled there. The decree of 10 August 1932 reversed the previous liberal measures and attempted to stem the growing unemployment generated by the incoming depression. A

Table 1.3 Distribution of immigrants by continent of origin, 1946–90 (%)

	1946	1954	1990
Europe	88.7	79.1	40.3
Africa	3.1	13.0	45.8
America	0.5	2.8	2.1
Asia	4.0	2.3	11.6
Total (million)	1.7	1.8	3.6

third wave of immigrants came in the 1960s as extensive infrastructure programmes demanded more hands than the native population could tender. In the first years of that decade, half a million *pieds noirs** (or ex-French colonists) resettled in the home country after Algerian independence (March 1962). Still this was not enough and Portuguese and Spanish workers came in throngs, soon followed by natives from the Maghreb (chiefly Algeria and Morocco). A second peak was reached in 1975 (7.3 per cent of the the labour force), one year after the government had officially ended its policy of encouraging 'economic' immigration.

Although official immigration is now restricted to a few tens of thousands a year (mainly on account of family reunification), the immigrant community has kept on growing in absolute and relative size (see Table 1.3). Since 1982, non-Europeans have constituted the majority of foreign immigrants on French soil, and with a fertility rate double that of Europeans, second-generation youths of North African origin (or *beurs** as they are commonly called) have become a sizeable and conspicuous group. French nationality was granted to two million permanent immigrants in the course of the century, but those of extra-European origin seem today little inclined to take it up and successive governments have tried to entice them to do so by various means. Perhaps this failure accounts for the fact that the foreign immigrant community today (five million people) looms so large in France as compared to neighbouring countries.

Where demography is concerned, the French, who adopted a different kind of distinct behaviour at the turn of the twentieth century,

---

* All (French) terms followed by an asterisk are succinctly explained in the Glossary at the end of the volume.

have returned to normality, or rather seem to have anticipated it. Their early experience with extensive birth control and the 'demographic transition' brought about a stagnation of their numbers which proved unconducive to economic growth and social progress. Nevertheless, they participated in the postwar baby boom and the following deceleration (sometimes referred to as 'baby crunch' or 'granddaddy boom'). Over the last twenty years, however, their fertility rate, although not guaranteeing the replacement of existing generations, has fallen markedly less than in other countries such as those of southern Europe, or even Scandinavia or Germany. The contribution of France's immigrant population seems indisputable in this regard. The future will tell if the fast-ageing population in one of the first secular societies of human history can be rejuvenated by its latest intake.

2. Whither French *joie-de-vivre*?

In 1930, Friedrich Sieburg published a widely read book with a title reminiscent of the German proverb 'Happy as God in France',[2] in which he praised what he perceived as the laid-back French attitude towards and sensible suspicion of the modern world's obsession with profit and efficiency. In a famous passage he described a small-town shopkeeper putting up the shutters very promptly at closing time to go and admire the sunset in spite of the vociferous queue at his door. Half a century later there could have been no more complete change of scenery. Fourastié started his famous *Trente glorieuses* (1979) by contrasting daily life in two apparently widely differing places which turned out to be the same one seen successively in 1946 and 1975. These changes appeared dramatic seen from behind the camera of film director Jacques Tati in the late 1950s/early 1960s, from the humane and friendly atmosphere of the traditional marketplace where the eponymous hero of *Mon Oncle* (1958) lived to the impersonal, concrete and cold reality of the robotic, empty existence of the characters in *Trafic* (1971). Although the causes of this leap into modernity are somewhat hard to fathom, France was not the only country to experience it and one could

---

[2] The title of the English translation was *Is God a Frenchman?* (London: Jonathan Cape, 1931).

certainly find similar nostalgia-inspired scenes in many a film of the Italian new realism school. The 'Golden Age' of European economic growth ushered in a 'truly European society' (Kaelble, 1980) and resulted in a profound convergence of living standards and lifestyles across European countries, a trend quickly attributed in France to the irresistible attraction of the American way of life and sometimes satirised as 'Americanisation'. This process of convergence affected virtually every aspect of individual and collective life; it transformed social hierarchies, working conditions, the working and living environment, family life and leisure, training and consumption patterns. The general rise in income levels blurred class identities, dissolved class distinctions and extended middle-class living standards to the majority of the working population. As far as labour income is concerned, the salary range (after tax) narrowed over much of the century, especially between the mid-1960s and the mid-1980s (1 to 4.1 in 1967, 1 to 3 in 1984). The trend was subsequently reversed and the gap has been widening since (1 to 6 in 1996). However, the standardisation of living conditions and lifestyles has proceeded, as is shown by the diffusion of working and living habits hitherto reserved either to the 'leisured class' or to a selective group of professionals, regarding dress and eating patterns as well as entertainment. This standardisation was brought about relatively quickly, by a phase of more intensive industrialisation followed by the seemingly unstoppable expansion of service activities (in and outside the tertiary sector). For the vast majority of French people, as in other advanced countries, the 'desk' has replaced the workbench, as Parkinson predicted.[3] Even in the mid-1960s, when farmers were still leaving agriculture in droves, the industrial sector ceased expanding, reaching a ceiling (also perceptible in other similar countries) of just under 40 per cent of the workforce and most new job creation was henceforth to take place in the service sector, reflecting in part a switch in people's consumption patterns towards traded and non-traded services.

As the proportion of manual labour was drastically reduced, so was, at least superficially, the amount of time that most people had to devote to earning a living. The recorded average annual working time shrank from upwards of 2,600 hours at the beginning of

[3] C. Northcote Parkinson, *In-laws and Outlaws* (London: John Murray, 1962).

Table 1.4 Distribution of workforce by sector, 1906–1998 (%)

Year	Agriculture	Industry	Services
1906	41.4	31.5	27.1
1931	32.1	36.2	31.7
1954	26.1	34.3	39.6
1974	10.6	38.5	50.9
1998	4.4	26.0	69.6

the century to under 2,000 hours in the 1950s and 1,500 today. From an individual perspective, the time alloted to gainful employment has also been curtailed at both ends of an individual's lifespan. Progressive extension of the school-leaving age to fourteen (1936) and sixteen (1959), as well as the growing enrolment of students in higher education, has delayed entry into the labour force. The emergence of mass unemployment in the 1980s also contributed to this. In 2000, as a result, barely 26 per cent of men and women in the 15–24 cohort were in employment (compared with 45 per cent in Britain and 46 per cent in Germany). At the other end of the spectrum, large segments of the ageing workforce have chosen to retire early and make up a growing constituency of senior citizens. In 1981, the official retirement age was lowered to sixty. But many public servants could already claim pension rights even earlier and pre-retirement schemes have been introduced for employees aged fifty or over facing redundancy and with few prospects of re-employment.[4] The transfer from the active to the inactive population, along with rising life expectancy, is continuously swelling pension costs and health expenditure. Because of the generous provisions introduced for statutory pensions in the 1970s, a pensioner household's annual earnings are now on average 20 per cent higher than those of households with at least one person in employment.

At the turn of the twenty-first century, France presents the familiar sight of a relatively dynamic society increasingly dominated by an ageing gerontocracy (a feature most apparent when considering

---

[4] In 2000, 37 per cent of the 55–64 age bracket were in employment compared to 51 per cent in the OECD and 66 per cent in Japan.

Table 1.5 Age distribution of French population (%)

Age	1901	1946	1995
under 20	34.4	29.5	26.8
20–60	53.0	54.5	53.5
over 60	12.6	16.0	19.7

politicians) while at the same time worshipping all the attributes of youth.

Thus, in this very 'postmodern' country, professional activity (or gainful employment) seems to have receded to a shorter proportion of people's lifetimes and to be interspersed with longer waiting periods (of training, retraining, unemployment and eventually early retirement): a person's working life appears much shorter but perhaps more intense at the same time. While working time has dwindled, employment has become an obsession; work demands less physical energy but far more mental energy, concentration, focus. People increasingly organise their personal life around their career and even temporary unemployment causes most people affected by it grave psychological and material disruptions. We have indeed come a long way from Sieburg's village shopkeeper.

The average French person's working and living environment has been as much transformed in the course of one generation or two as have been his or her working conditions. To get the full picture, one naturally needs to step off the tourist trail which has (rightfully) made France the world's favourite holiday destination. The impressions expressed by the young American hero of Benoît Duteurtre's recent novel *Voyage en France* (2001) is of garish, vulgar industrial estates, drab shopping malls, fast-food outlets and ubiquitous traffic congestion – much the same as where he comes from.

In the past fifty years the supposedly traditional French way of life has all but disappeared and the circumstances of most French people have converged onto a Western standard. This becomes apparent when examining the dominant environment of French daily life.

Sociologically, rising incomes and rural migrations have buoyed the suburban middle classes. Entire segments of the former working class were *de facto* included in the middle class during the 1970s and 1980s. In 1911, 66 per cent of the population still lived in the country and France was one of the least urbanised countries in Western Europe: there were only fifteen cities with over 100,000 inhabitants against forty-nine in Britain and forty-five in Germany. By 1990 the share of the urban population had risen to 75.3 per cent of the total. Definitions changed, however, in the meantime and so did the urban living environment. Up to the Second World War, middle-sized nineteenth-century provincial *bourgs* (market towns) dominated France's urban landscape. Increasingly since then, urban settlement has involved the continuous expansion of metropolitan areas in the form of sprawling suburbs (a phenomenon known to geographers as 'rurbanisation'). Until the 1960s the urban population, as well as the industrial areas, were concentrated geographically in the north-eastern half of the country (north of an imaginary line stretching from Normandy to Marseilles), where industrial build-up naturally attracted rural and other migrants. Since then, developments have been more segmented or complex. Older industrial regions like the Lorraine and Nord have shed older residents and failed to attract new; in the greater Paris area, population shifted first from the urban centre to the immediate suburbs (nicknamed the 'little crown' or 'red belt' on account of their predominantly left-wing vote) and then to the more remote 'great crown'. To the surprise of British or American visitors, most French inner cities are well preserved and (apart from the central districts almost wholly taken up by corporate offices) are still inhabited by their local residents. But a yawning gap is developing between the 'civilised' metropolises and *le désert français*, between the agreeable if conventional *lotissements** (middle-class residential areas) and the drab *cités** (popular housing estates), between the hectic pace of commuting and the workplace and the forced inactivity and lack of purpose of those kept out of it. This tension has fuelled stress, a growing sense of insecurity, and an 'existentialist'[5] quest for a new identity among the French who have become the world's largest consumers of tranquillisers – as well they might: a Frenchman (Laborit) patented the first brand.

---

[5] A reference to the basic tenet of 'existentialism' according to which a philosphy of life can be grounded only in life experience (cf. Sartre, 1946).

Chapter 2
French economic performance in international perspective

By most accounts France 'held its own' among the group of industrialised countries: its overall economic performance was 'commendable' – if not optimal – over the twentieth century. The fourth largest economy at the time of the Paris universal exhibition of 1900, it had more or less regained this position by the time of the fall of the Berlin wall in 1989. In terms of sheer economic potential, the demotion from the pedestal of 'great nation' had occurred already in the nineteenth century. In terms of individual incomes, the French have managed to keep their living standards in the league of advanced countries, although their level of disposable income did not catch up with that of the Americans (and other non-European advanced countries) until the 1970s. For the greater part of the century, therefore, although nominally part of the 'rich world', the French enjoyed living standards markedly inferior to those across the Atlantic. The leap into the affluent society took place during the first postwar period (1945–73), affectionately known to the French as 'Les Trente Glorieuses'.[1] In terms of demography, economic make-up and wealth, this period constitutes the main watershed and would invite us to split our examination of the century down the middle (all the more so as French 'capitalism' then took a marked turn towards 'socialism'). But as much as for the emergence of the consumer society, the twentieth century may be remembered in future for the massive destruction of human life and property in two world wars. It is therefore probably simpler to consider the French growth record through four separate periods of unequal duration:

---

[1] 'Thirty glorious years': from the title of a bestseller published in 1979 by economist Jean Fourastié, who took the 'trois glorieuses' days of the 1830 revolution (28–29–30 July) as a metaphor.

Table 2.1 Average annual growth rate of GNP in the twentieth century (%)

	1900–1913	1914–1950	1950–1973	1973–1998
France	**1.63**	**1.15**	**5.05**	**2.1**
Germany	2.83	1.06	5.68	1.76
Italy	1.94	1.49	5.64	2.28
UK	1.90	1.19	2.93	2.0
EU 12	2.14	1.16	4.65	2.03

the Belle Epoque (1900–1913), the wars and interwar years (1914–1945), the first postwar period (1945–73) and finally the period up to 1998. France performed marginally worse than Western Europe until 1950, slightly better during the 'Golden Age', and aligned its performance on the European average during the last quarter of the century (see Table 2.1).

1. Then and now

The 'Belle Epoque' (which was so labelled in retrospect after the ordeal of the First World War) is generally viewed as the 'springboard' of French postwar growth, mainly on account of an influential study published in 1972 (Carré et al., 1975 for the English edition), and a database constructed from the 1896 industrial census. But this period can as justifiably be considered as the continuation of nineteenth-century trends rather than the anticipation of later developments.

The contention that France was in this period on a path to more intensive modernisation and industrialisation has many adherents (Caron, 1979; Beltran and Griset, 1994; Barjot, 1995).[2] On the strength of the expansionary cycle of the first decade of the century, the country was apparently poised to reconquer her former position as a frontline economy, had this process not been cut short by the outbreak of the First World War. Unfortunately, the evidence on which this assertion rests is open to conflicting interpretation.

[2] The majority of French economic historians see it as their duty to defend the past economic record of their country in all circumstances (and sometimes in the teeth of the evidence).

On the positive side, the macroeconomic evidence suggests a resumption of rural migration to the cities and a spectacular rebound in industrial growth following the lethargy of the 'Great Depression' (1873–96) to a rate of 4.2 per cent per annum between 1905 and 1913. Upon closer inspection, however, the magnitude of the spurt, which only really took hold after the 1907–8 recession, was probably more modest. However, this period did witness intense activity on various fronts: in addition to a wave of mergers and takeovers in established industries, advances were made in new and promising technologies such as motorcars and aeroplanes, photography and film, and also the manufacture of compressed gases, aluminium smelting and public works. Gifted scientists teamed with committed amateurs to make important technological breakthroughs and launch new fashions. However, French product innovation in this period invariably represented expensive gadgets or luxury goods aimed at a narrow range of customers, national as well as international. Many new entrants in these production lines were able to secure profitable niches, at least for a time, but found it very hard to expand their customer base or break into the virtuous circle of cost reduction and economies of scale. The automobile industry is a case in point: in 1900, French manufacturers held the first rank in the world, but they lagged markedly behind British and German (not to mention American) competitors by 1929.

In spite of an array of quality products known the world over, the bulk of French agriculture and industry struggled through difficult times. While agriculture was (albeit imperfectly) sheltered from foreign competition by tariffs, it stumbled from one crisis to the next and industry's largest sectors were subjected to drastic reorganisation and some closures. 'Second industrial revolution' technology in chemicals, metal alloys and electrical engineering developed only timidly. Isolated critics such as Charles Mourre and Pierre Baudin warned that France was on its way down the slippery slope of economic decline. But the majority of French politicians, as relayed by the media in the nationalist atmosphere of this period, were complacent about the actual strength and potential of the country's economy.

The prestige of French culture and language abroad somehow concealed the harsher realities which had developed out of 'nationalist economic policies' introduced at the beginning of the

Table 2.2 Productivity measured by GNP per employee per year (USA = 100)

	1913	1950	1973	1998
France	**56.0**	**47.5**	**78.4**	**91.1**
Germany	58.7	39.1	65.4	72.7
Italy	40.6	37.0	63.0	76.5
UK	84.8	65.8	66.2	73.5

Third Republic some thirty years before and continued ever since. These were intended to promote self-sufficiency, isolate the domestic economy from outward influence, slow down urbanisation and limit industrialisation. By the early 1900s, it was becoming obvious that France had not taken full advantage of its precocious industrial advances and integration in the world economy; opportunities had been missed and incentives thwarted. By 1913, the country's economy looked more like Italy's or Austria's than Britain's which it had earlier shadowed. In the outsize traditional sector (55 per cent of the population lived in rural districts of fewer than 2,000 people), farming's capacity to feed the country's population fell increasingly short of demand; nearly a million farms of fewer than two acres found it hard enough to survive, let alone supply outside markets.

Industrial growth was hampered by the narrowness of the domestic market: small self-sufficient farmers, with a strong tendency toward hoarding cash or purchasing land, did not make promising and reliable customers. Traditional consumer industries, a majority of them still carried on in small units or *ateliers*,* catered to local needs as well as to a discriminating but limited urban middle class. The development of services was limited by the resilience of the traditional economy and the slow pace of industrialisation. Precious resources were diverted into colonial enterprise and risky financial commitments abroad (in Russia and Austria-Hungary). The exertions and outcome of the the First World War were to serve as a severe audit of French economic weaknesses.

2. Creative destruction?

From an economic and technological viewpoint the period 1914–45 constitutes a stumbling block in European history. It may reasonably be asked what shape technological progress would have assumed had it not been for the resultant massive diversion of energy and resources from the civilian to the military defence sector.

During the period covering the two world wars and the intervening twenty years' truce, France, like most European countries, experienced very slow growth (Table 2.2). Between the wars, improvements in living conditions for the vast majority of the population were barely perceptible although national income rose at little over 1 per cent per annum. In the aggregate, most of the gains were concentrated in the late 1920s and to some extent eroded subsequently. As in Germany and the US, business was relatively buoyant in the second half of that decade, while living standards, as well as spirits, collapsed during the depression years of the 1930s.

In view of the terrible destruction brought about by the first 'mechanised' conflict in European history, it is little short of extraordinary that the nation recovered at all, certainly so relatively quickly.[3] By 1924, production, agricultural and industrial, had recovered to its prewar level, though it would take another six years to complete the comprehensive reconstruction programme on the northern and eastern borders (thirteen *départements** in total) which had been either looted by the Germans or subjected to intense bombardment.[4] While the generations which suffered the horror and misery of the war never fully recovered from it, the conflict also left deep scars in the economic landscape of the country.

The cannon-merchant theory of capitalism contends that military conflicts can have positive effects on economic growth, more specifically on industrial expansion. This is a narrow view of their consequences. In so far as war caused vast human and material destruction, it certainly speeded up consumption and therefore production of basic necessities, as well as the more obvious supply of military equipment being destroyed at a fast pace. In addition, the exigencies of armed conflict typically bend production systems as well as technological innovation towards the manufacture of armaments and other equipment and away from civilian production. Finally, war is likely to increase the short-termism of

---

[3] Demographically the war made no difference one way or the other, as the population of Alsace-Lorraine, annexed in 1919, made up for the loss of life in the war.
[4] In 1919, Parliament decided to finance the reconstruction of buildings on the basis of the existing stock as on 1 August 1914.

decision-makers and to leave in its wake deep financial as well as structural imbalances.

In France, as in neighbouring countries, the financial and monetary troubles of the interwar period originated in fiscal (mis)management during the war. Not apparent at first, the full effects of the fiscal extravaganza initiated to pay for the war were to hit governments and taxpayers with a vengeance. Despite the introduction of a tax on wartime profits in 1917 and of personal income tax in 1914, the French wartime governments relied only marginally on taxation to finance the war effort.[5] Instead, they resorted to borrowing, in the form of either advances from the Banque de France,* or medium- and longer-term loans from allied governments and banks (mostly British and American). But above all they swamped the domestic market with national defence bonds which swelled the floating debt: by 1920 interest payments were already swallowing 26 per cent of the government budget. Fortunately, price inflation – the result of the runaway issue of banknotes, treasury bills and other means of payment – soon reduced this debt. In 1921, 1924 and 1929 the government negotiated the rescheduling of its foreign debt. As the gold convertibility of the franc (and therefore its parity with foreign currencies) had been suspended on 1 August 1914, many *rentiers** were caught in a trap: by 1929 government bonds had lost 62 per cent of their value. By contrast, holders of more liquid assets were free to transfer them abroad in anticipation of an impending official devaluation – which eventually came in 1926. Capital flight was especially extensive (and, to political decision-makers, worrying) in 1924 and 1936.

These financial uncertainties were not conducive to sound business activity. Economic growth and structural change proceeded only by fits and starts after 1919. Aggregate GNP figures were only slightly higher in 1938 than in 1913. In the meantime the labour force had shrunk by a million (despite the annexation of Alsace-Lorraine) and labour inputs had been further reduced by limitations on working hours (forty-eight-hour week in 1919; forty-hour week in 1936). While industrial output stagnated between

---

[5] The payment of the profits tax, delayed by bureaucracy, was further eroded by inflation.

1929 and 1938, agriculture crawled upward at a rate of 0.4 per cent per annum.

3. A miracle by any other name (1945–1973)

Just like the pre-1914 'Belle Epoque', the Trente Glorieuses,[6] the French version of the European 'Golden Age', received its name in retrospect: public opinion and decision-makers did not feel any special sense of bliss or glory at the time. The expression was coined during the succeeding period of economic troubles and introspection.

France having experienced in swift succession the ordeal of German invasion and occupation and finally liberation by the Allies, her reconstruction prospects looked dim by both past and current standards. While the death toll had been lower than in the previous conflict, it is no exaggeration to say that the country had been bled dry. On VE day, while close to a million men were still held in Nazi PoW camps, it is reckoned that the war had cost a quarter of the nation's total wealth (three times as much as the first war); a million dwellings had been destroyed as well as large amounts of infrastructure, especially railways and rolling stock, bridges and ports. War indemnities paid to the German occupying authorities and plants and equipment seized by them had forced the closure of many production lines. Agricultural and industrial output were at a fraction of their prewar levels (60 and 44 per cent respectively). Rationing (only suspended in 1949) and shortages were widespread; inflation ran high, fed as it was by the huge imbalance between perceived needs and available resources (made worse by the black market) and a display of accumulated wealth by certain categories of producers (some war profiteers but also hoarders of basic foodstuffs).

It took some time before the economy was put in order. To the average Frenchwoman 1947 was worse, in terms of calorie intake and disposable income, than any of the war years. In 1948, the ERP (or 'Marshall Plan') and the skilful stabilisation plan by PM René Mayer set the French economy on its path to recovery. The influx of American aid and the relaxing of price controls progressively reduced shortages; by the end of the year industrial production had

[6] Cf. note 1 above.

Table 2.3 Average annual growth rate of GNP among OECD countries, 1950–2000 (%)

	1950–9	1960–73	1973–9	1979–90	1990–9
France	**4.6**	**5.8**	**2.8**	**2.5**	**1.6**
Germany	8.6	4.4	2.3	2.0	2.1
UK	3.0	3.2	1.5	2.1	1.9
Italy	5.5	5.3	2.6	2.5	1.2
USA	3.5	3.9	2.6	2.6	2.7
OECD	5.1	4.7	2.6	2.6	2.5

regained its prewar level (equalling in 1949 its interwar peak of 1929)[7] and most remaining restrictions were progressively lifted. Thereafter productivity gains triggered a spectacular catching-up process. While strong economic growth could be expected in the period of reconstruction, its continuation and acceleration were by no means predictable thereafter. In fact, the reconstruction effort fed directly into the 'affluent society'. Between 1951 and 1973 growth averaged 5.4 per cent per annum, a far higher rate than either at the beginning of the century (1.8 per cent) or during the interwar period (0.9 per cent). This performance was comparable to that of Italy and West Germany, and better than that of Britain or the USA at the time. Furthermore, it clearly accelerated from the 1950s (4.6 per cent) to the 1960s (5.5 per cent) and the early 1970s (5.6 per cent). It was so regular from one year to the next that observers proclaimed that the business cycle had been broken (although overheating spells are clearly identifiable in 1953, 1957, 1963 and 1968).

This 'great leap forward' was engineered by continuous productivity gains sustained by a more efficient use of resources. On the one hand, labour input, constrained until 1962 by a stable working population, was boosted by a relaxation of statutory restrictions on working hours (the forty-hour week introduced in 1936);[8] on the other, there was a massive shift in resources from traditional,

---

[7] By comparison it had taken six years after the First World War for industrial production to recover its prewar level.
[8] In the mid-1950s, the average working week in industry was typically 45.2 hours.

stagnant activities (mainly agriculture) to the modern sectors of industry and urban services. Simultaneously, productive investment, fuelled by a surge in capital accumulation, boosted worker productivity: in the aggregate, capital formation went from 13.3 per cent of GNP in 1959 to 15.1 per cent in 1973. By the time of the 1973 oil crisis, French workers, who had been only a third as productive as their American counterparts in 1950, were fast closing the gap, especially when productivity was measured on an hourly basis.

This expansion was, until the gradual dismantling of trade restrictions in the late 1960s (a commitment agreed to at the Kennedy round of GATT and in the Treaty of Rome), as in other European countries, largely 'domestic'. World (or even regional) trade liberalisation took another decade to materialise and even longer to bear fruit. Gradually, however, French producers switched from the protected market of the *franc zone** to more competitive markets in Western Europe and North America. At the same time, postwar economic development remained under the heavy hand of the state: the government inherited a vast arsenal of policy instruments from the interwar and war years which were used to shape the reconstruction and ensuing expansion. This was effected by setting priorities (planning), building new infrastructures, and adopting active monetary policies (credit and price controls) and industrial policies.

While the period 1950–73 emerges as one of relative price stability when compared to the country's past record (between 1928 and 1949 eleven devaluations were carried out, eroding 99 per cent of the value of the currency), inflation remained endemic and the inflation differential with France's main partners forced periodic adjustments of the value of the franc. Governments used wage and price freezes repeatedly and imposed credit squeezes and restraints on demand, but never managed to eliminate it completely. Inflation, as in Britain and more so in Italy, was in fact built into the country's redistributive system. With the real cost of raw materials falling worldwide, prices of goods and services drifted as a result of rising taxation, uncompetitive organisation of distribution channels and income-securing behaviour. However, this situation had the enormous advantage of eroding collusion between government and business, transferring wealth from liquidity holders to property owners, and improving returns on capital assets, especially for firms.

Figure 2.1 The French inflation record, 1920–90

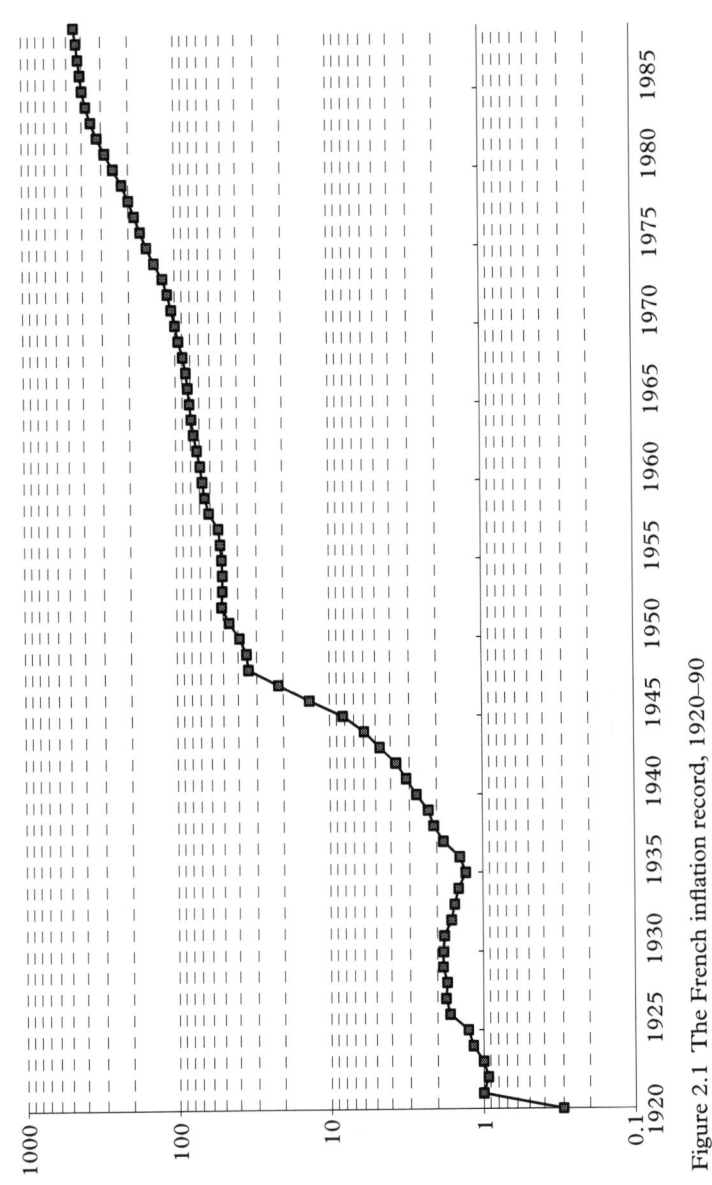

Table 2.4 The achievement of the 'Trente Glorieuses'

	1946	1975
Total population (millions)	40.5	52.6
Life expectancy (years)	55.9	70.2
Infant mortality (‰)	84.4	13.8
Participation rate (per cent)	51.4	41.4
Average annual hours worked	2100	1875
GNP per capita (1938 = 100)	87	320
Purchasing power of average wage	125	420
Homes built annually (thsds)	65	570
with private bathroom (%)	5	70.3
with telephone (%)	5	25
with refrigerator (%)	3	91
Private cars (millions)	1.0	15.3

Despite (or perhaps because of) creeping inflation, living standards dramatically improved during the whole period. True, this was not directly concomitant with economic expansion, but the time it took for the growth of GNP to translate into palpable increases of disposable income was much shorter than during earlier periods of expansion. On a rough calculation, average disposable income in the mid-1970s was nearly three times that at the beginning of the 1950s (not taking into account relative differences in price movements). Between 1959 and 1973 private consumption, growing at a healthy 4.25 per cent per annum, almost doubled (+80%). Because economic growth was so strong, pervasive and regular, its fruits came to be shared by the vast majority of the (working) population: the share of labour in national income rose at the expense of capital. This was the result of the political settlement concluded immediately after the war, which gave employees some clear advantages over employers, including improved work contracts, union representatives on *comités d'entreprise** (works councils) and collective bargaining, as well as the *de facto* indexation of wages to prices.

The welfare state (set up in 1945) also played a role in improving living standards: social transfers which represented one fifth of total income in 1952 reached one third in 1977 (Piketti, 2001). This last observation has led some observers to contend that this improvement was, to a large extent, the result of the new balance of power established at the Liberation.* Paradoxically, a sizeable share of contemporary public opinion refused to believe that any such improvement was actually taking place. As Communist doctrines still shaped representations and aspirations,[9] what came to be criticised at the end of the 1960s was not so much the incompleteness of prosperity as its very reality and meaning. 'You can't fall in love with a growth rate' was one of the slogans of student demonstrators in the Latin Quarter* during the May 1968 uprising. Little did the demonstrators know that within a mere seven years, their aspirations would be fulfilled beyond their dreams and the economy would grind to a halt.

4. Oil crisis and 'phoney' recovery

With hindsight the period following the 1973 oil crisis does not compare favourably with the 'thirty glorious years' of reconstruction and expansion (1945–75). Growth rates were dramatically curtailed during the second period as compared with the first, leaving growing numbers of people out of the labour market. One observer has gone so far as to label it the 'thirty pitiful years' of stagflation and bungled opportunities (Baverez, 1998). Today the French economy, which stabilised at a lower level in the 1980s, has yet to undergo full recovery. To be sure, the descent into stagnation was very gradual: the 'automatic stabilisers' instituted by the managed economy initially cushioned the worst effects of the 'double whammy' (1973 and 1979) oil crisis. It was only in the medium term that they became manifest.

For the West, the quadrupling of crude oil prices in September 1973, coupled with the collapse of the Bretton Woods system in 1971, ushered in a new phase of capitalist development. On the one hand it burdened Western economies with higher fuel costs – in France, for a ten-year period well into the 1980s. On the other, it served as a catalyst for the emergence of hitherto unsuspected but growing problems of adaptation to a new global division of labour and to recent technological change. Economic policy instruments

---

[9] Until the 1970s, the French Communist Party (PCF) regularly polled between 20 and 25 per cent of the electorate (except in the 1959 general election).

and institutions designed in the postwar years proved increasingly ill-suited to deal with the spill-over effects of globalisation, as regional and multilateral trade agreements painfully obtained in the 1960s created a more open trade environment and impinged on national comparative advantages.

The consecutive oil crises of 1973 and 1979 brought about an immediate increase in the country's external fuel bill – equivalent to 3 per cent of GNP in 1973 and rising to 5 per cent in the early 1980s. Owing to the deterioration of trade conditions, the oil crisis unsettled the balance of payments and indirectly accelerated inflation, which had already gathered momentum in the early 1970s, towards unprecedented highs. Price inflation leapt to 15 per cent in 1974 and hovered around 10 per cent for the rest of the decade only to experience a rebound in the early 1980s. The acceleration can be interpreted as the outcome of conflicting 'beggar my neighbour' strategies used by various social and professional groups to shift the burden of increased fuel costs onto others. On the whole, firms bore the brunt of this, which increased their production costs but reduced their competitiveness – as demonstrated by Prime Minister Chirac's introduction of the *taxe professionnelle** in 1976.

After GNP fell in 1975 (by 0.5 per cent), the economy was kept on a growth path of 2.8 per cent until 1980 by a combination of demand management and incomes policy. The recession was put off in the hope of minimising its impact – a strategy strikingly similar to that of the 1930s. The 1981–2 counter-cyclical boom engineered by the incoming Socialist government was intended to break the spiral of stagflation; it resulted only in further enlargement of the budget and trade deficits. The productive system nurtured in the first postwar period was increasingly at odds with emerging tastes and needs. Golden age consumption patterns (domestic appliances for instance) had reached saturation point and were failing to sustain demand for domestic manufactures. Conversely, increased openness and international competition dented French firms' market share both at home and abroad, inducing downsizing and outsourcing which would feed a long-lasting process of de-industrialisation. As earnings kept growing faster than GNP, while productivity fell behind, productive investment bore the worst of the crunch: net capital formation was virtually nil between 1973 and 1979 and it would take another seven years to return to pre-crisis levels. The standard interpretation emphasises the role of rising labour costs (real wages kept rising at a healthy 3 per cent per annum) in bringing down corporate profitability (which halved between the 1970s and the 1980s), increasing firms' indebtedness and financial costs. This led to a dramatic contraction of investment as firms cut down on productive capacity.

Until 1983, in spite of the seemingly unstoppable rise in unemployment, automatic stabilisers, in the guise of rising public expenditure, mitigated the full effect of the crisis. In March 1983, after three consecutive devaluations, the Socialist government decided to turn its back on Keynesian pump-priming policies. Successive *plans de relance** had only resulted in widening both the trade and the budget deficits. Existing credit and exchange controls clearly were not succeeding in stemming capital outflows. It appeared that pursuing this type of policy would necessitate further moves towards isolating the French economy from the world in general and France's European partners in particular. Jacques Delors, then Minister of Finance, introduced a *plan de rigueur** containing measures aimed at setting the economy on a course of disinflation, restructuring and a balance of payments more conducive to European integration.

Consequently, growth momentarily slumped and settled at a much lower average than during either the 'Golden Age' or the 1970s. With the return of the business cycle, growth also became more fickle. Between 1981 and 1985 GNP grew at an average of 1.5 per cent per annum before reviving in the 'boom' of 1986–1989, when it reached 3.1 per cent. But for most of the 1990s, French performance, at 1.2 per cent annually, was at the bottom of the EU league which collectively exhibited 1.6 per cent annual growth from 1991 to 1997. Admittedly, France did relatively well during the ensuing boom (1998–2000) but this was relatively short-lived: in 2001 the economy resumed the crawling pace of the early 1990s. Interest rates set by the ECB seem to have been at least partly responsible for slow growth in 'Euroland'.

From 1983 onwards priority was given to rehabilitating the currency and re-establishing the balance of payments. This was perceived as a precondition for restoring some necessary optimism to the economic outlook and creating a stable environment

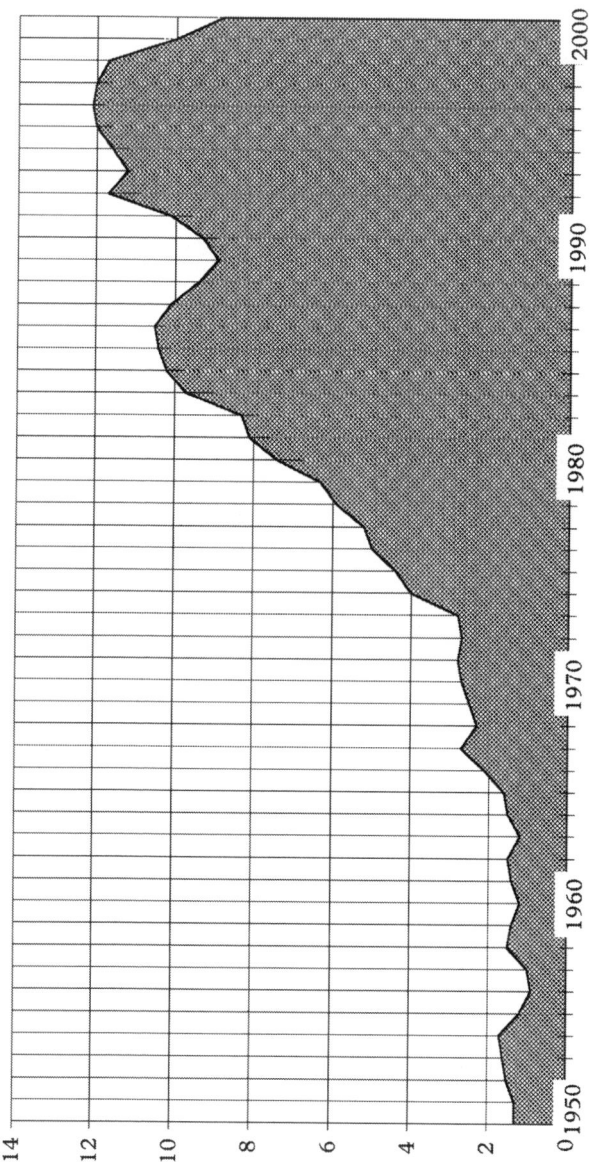

Figure 2.2 French unemployed as a percentage of the working population, 1950–2000 (ILO definition)

for corporate investment decisions. By 1989, France's inflation differential with its EU partners was finally eliminated; in fact, more than 80 per cent of the gap had been eliminated by the end of 1985. Bringing inflation under control progressively restored the return on assets, interest rates and firm profitability to 'normal', pre-oil-crisis levels.

The most visible effect of this policy change was felt after 1986 when the centre-right returned to power and took decisive steps in deregulation. Together these measures brought about a surge in unemployment. There were 1.5 million unemployed (6 per cent of the working population) when the Socialists came to power in 1981; even after the 1988 peak, in 1990, there were still 2.2 million; in 1997 unemployment reached an all-time high of 3.2 million (12.1 per cent). By the end of the century, the IT boom had resulted in the creation of 0.85 million jobs, which brought unemployment down to the 1990 level. But France still had one of the highest unemployment rates in the EU. High unemployment as well as hidden unemployment (in the form of subsidised jobs) reflect negatively on participation rates. In an effort to curb unemployment, successive governments set up schemes to delay the entry of young adults into the workforce and other schemes to encourage the early retirement of redundant unskilled workers. As a result participation rates in the 15–24 and 55–64 cohorts fell sharply (from 47.5 to 28 per cent and from 53.6 to 36.7 per cent respectively between 1980 and 1997). Both these categories contribute to a widening gap in participation rates as compared with the EU average: fewer adults in the 24–55 age bracket are unemployed but they have to work harder so as to sustain a growing number of dependants. In this context, greater labour market flexibility would obviously pave the way to fuller capacity utilisation. But a wide coalition of vested interests are still opposed to any such move.

Chapter 3
France and the wider world

The greater openness to and integration of a nation's economy with the rest of the world is widely regarded by economists as the key factor in optimal economic development and performance. The free flow of goods, ideas, labour and capital constitutes the means by which countries can exploit successfully the ever-changing international division of labour and develop the specialisation best suited to their resource endowment. Globalisation was launched when Europeans started to establish regular communications with other continents, from the sixteenth century onwards. It was given a decisive boost in the nineteenth century, when the capabilities of both production and transport were enhanced by the technology of the industrial revolution. Although devoid of any major European conflict, this century gave birth to nationalist ideologies which were to have far-reaching consequences. In Europe they spawned two destructive major wars which seriously disrupted the trend towards a more integrated world economy. These originated in Europe and were essentially fought on European soil. In both of them, France occupied centre stage.

Conversely, economic as well as political competition among European nation-states has always been a major feature of European history and may constitute a key to understanding the continent's precocious and continuing success (Rosenberg & Birdzell, 1984). But in the short term, the period from 1914 to 1945 (also referred to as Europe's twentieth-century 'Thirty years' war') has caused immense destruction, suffering and lost opportunities – despite the League of Nations' efforts to secure greater international co-operation. Breakthroughs in economic integration and international

Table 3.1 Degree of openness (proportion of exports in GNP) (%)

	1913	1929	1950	1973	1998
France	7.8	8.6	7.6	15.2	28.7
Germany	16.1	12.8	6.2	23.8	38.9
UK	17.5	13.3	11.3	14.0	25.0
World	7.9	9.0	5.5	10.5	17.2

co-operation since the middle of the nineteenth century were reversed, commodity trade collapsed and financial flows dried up; governments introduced authoritarian allocation of resources to curb competition – some even feared at the time that this would usher in a 'new dark age' (Churchill). Fortunately, the second postwar reconstruction paved the way to a restoration of international integration and co-operation.

France has shared in this common history. For most of the century France, like many other countries, had to put 'defence before prosperity' and devote considerable resources and effort to actively protecting its territory and national interests. The prospect of yet another conflict of cataclysmic proportions in the immediate postwar period reinforced the tendency to tighten, rather than discard, the regulatory corset imposed during and between the two world wars. By the end of the 1960s, however, multilateral agreements (GATT) and regional co-operation (EEC) paved the way for a more outward-looking economy. By the mid-1980s this trend had become irresistible as financial transactions were fully liberalised. 'Fortress France' has thus escaped the vicious circle of nationalism, protectionism and colonialism which doubtless hampered its economic development in the first half of the twentieth century. Despite recurring cries to 'control and curb unbridled globalisation' (from government ministers attending the 'social summit' in Porto Alegre, Brazil), growing openness seems to be the only way to ensure the country's continued prosperity. At the close of the century, France's degree of openness was over three times its 1929 level (see Table 3.1).

1. Domestic vs. trade-induced growth?

Small countries, given their narrow domestic markets and their limited range of resources and production, have no choice, if they want to expand, but to open their borders to outside influences (the free flow of people, goods, capital and technology) and specialise in order to capture foreign customers. Relatively large countries, by contrast, can entertain the illusion of 'going it alone': in theory a larger domestic market can absorb, and a multitude of economic agents can supply, a greater variety of goods. Thus industrialisation in the USA relied essentially on the domestic market and proceeded initially behind high tariff barriers. Conversely, the small economies of Western Europe have either thrived on a traditionally open stance (Denmark, the Netherlands, Belgium) or experienced prolonged periods of stagnation (Portugal, Ireland).

In the nineteenth century France had to adapt from an initial 'great nation' status to being a medium-size country at a time when continued industrial development was making goods, processes and services increasingly sophisticated and complementary. Concurrently, the parliamentary regime adopted by the country after 1870 offered more room for manœuvre to organised interest groups eager to introduce restrictive practices so as to limit outside competition. A policy 'to protect national labour' was officially embraced after the Méline* tariff of 1892 put an end to the episode of trade liberalisation opened by the Anglo-French treaty of 1860.[1] Consolidated in 1910, restored in 1928, reinforced from 1931 and again in 1949, protectionism endured until the breakthrough of the Kennedy round of GATT (1960–1) and the commitment to lower EEC 'internal' trade barriers (July 1962). Tariff protection enjoyed such longevity because of the inherent intricacy of the tariff: most of its deleterious effects were either hidden, diluted or cushioned because a large number of sheltered industries could thrive or subsist in a relatively closed environment.

For most of the past hundred years, therefore, relative isolation from the outside world has been a dominant feature, although it was

---

[1] Protectionist measures for manufacturing had already been introduced in 1881.

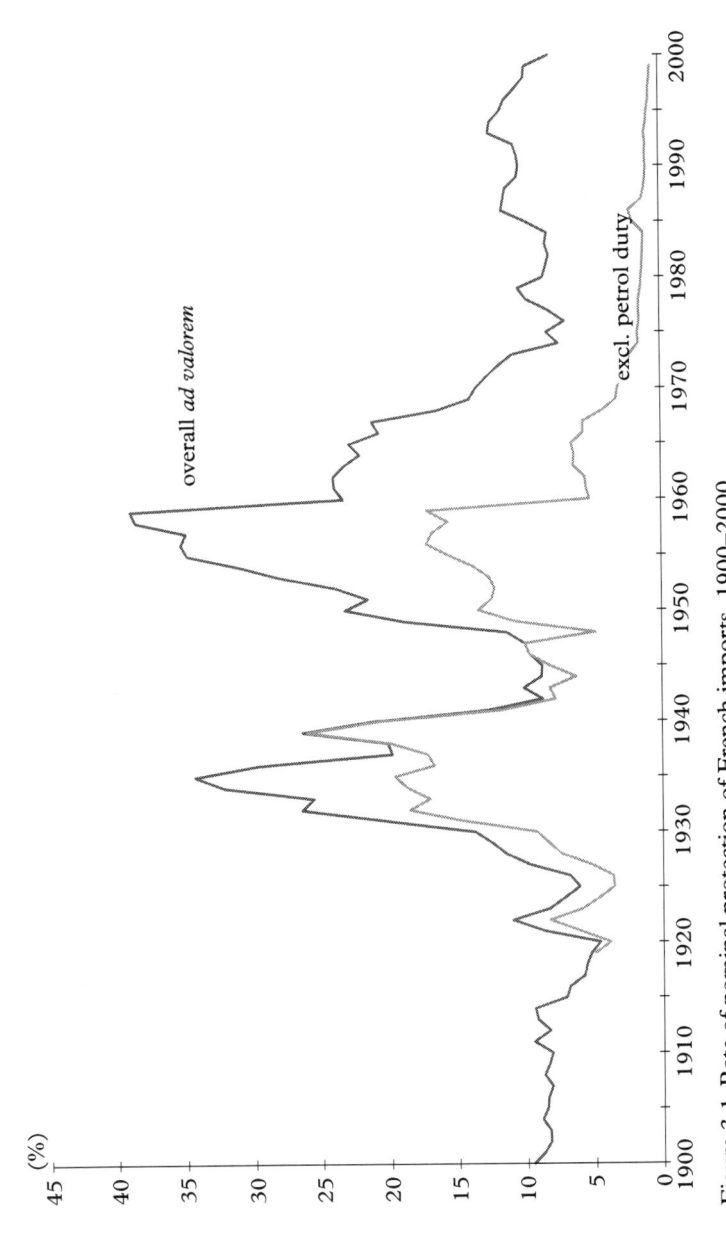

Figure 3.1 Rate of nominal protection of French imports, 1900–2000
Source: Annuaire Statistique de la France, 1900–2000.

Table 3.2 Simple linear regression impact of French trade openness on economic growth (%)

Year	Openness Rate[1]	Annual growth rate Actual	Predicted	Residuals
1900–9	17.7	2.27	2.20	0.07
1910–14	17.0	1.89	2.28	−0.39
1919–29	11.7	4.43	2.90	1.50
1930–9	10.0	0.63	3.10	−2.50
1945–9	8.0	2.16	3.34	−1.18
1950–9	9.8	3.85	3.13	0.77
1960–9	10.5	4.98	3.04	1.96
1970–9	15.7	3.10	2.43	0.67
1980–9	18.9	2.02	2.06	−0.06
1990–9	18.1	1.30	2.15	−0.85

[1] Exports as a share of GNP.
Source: Maddison, 2001.

less pronounced before the First World War than in the interwar period and the 1950s (Figure 3.1). The opening up of the economy dates only from the 1970s; by 1980 the openness rate (measured by the ratio of exports to GNP) had finally climbed back to its pre-1914 level (see Table 3.1). This delay partly accounts for the contradiction observed today between the country's successful integration in the world economy and the popularity of vociferous denunciations of globalisation.

Though a number of alternatives ('second-best choices') have been offered to the recommended policy of outright trade liberalisation, the existence of a positive relationship between a country's openness to trade and investment and economic growth is seldom questioned. But it is only to be expected that the empirical measurement of this relationship must be far from straightforward. It depends on the adequacy of the available data – and is affected by the impossibility of devising feasible counterfactuals.

In the French case, however, a cursory examination of national accounts statistics suggests such a relationship: it took sixty years for GNP per capita to double under protectionism (1900–60), but only twenty for it to double again after trade liberalisation set in. If we break down French growth and openness by decade, the correlation is weak but positive. It appears to be strongest in the first and last decades of the century. In between, the record suggests little could have been gained, in terms of either market share or growth performance, from adopting a freer trade stance, given the deeply distorted trade flows in the rest of the world.

The data lend themselves to a variety of interpretations which point to both the weakness and the fragility of France's comparative advantages. Firstly, wars and periods of prolonged recession had a stifling effect on foreign trade and investment, which took a long time to recover. Perhaps these stand among the longest-lasting effects of modern war. Second, it is obvious that changing outside circumstances have influenced both the policy options and their outcome. Raising tariff barriers in an increasingly open world economy prevents a country from reaping the benefits of enhanced specialisation; conversely, maintaining relatively free trade or moderate protection in the face of increasing market segmentation can have deleterious effects. In the field of international competition such trade strategies must be coherent, well informed, carefully designed and introduced at the right juncture. Most policies involving restrictive trade measures insist on the benefits accruing to the first mover, since the effect rapidly wears off. During the 1930s depression, France, whose trade barriers were already relatively high, failed to reap the advantages that Britain drew from the introduction of a protective tariff in 1932. Finally, tariff duties on imports represent only the tip of a submerged iceberg of trade restrictions which after the Second World War increasingly took the form of 'non-tariff barriers'. A more sophisticated form of protectionism, entangled in a web of regulations and agreements designed to discourage competitors, was nurtured during the period of reconstruction in the 1950s; it only began to be dismantled under pressure from the EU and GATT (later the WTO) in recent decades. To some extent, foreign trade regimes have reflected the competitive conditions prevailing in the domestic economy, as well as outside. In this respect, it is not irrelevant that internal competition law, almost unheard-of before, was designed and strengthened (in retail trade for instance) in the 1960s, at the very time that the French economy was opening to outside trade and investment flows.

Table 3.3 Share of world manufactured exports, 1913–98 (%)

	1913	1929	1937	1950	1973	1998
US	13.7	21.7	20.5	26.6	15.1	10.5
Japan	2.5	4.1	7.4	3.4	13.1	9.9
Germany	19.9	15.5	16.5	7.0	22.3	12.7
France	**14.9**	**11.6**	**6.2**	**9.6**	**9.3**	**6.2**
UK	31.8	23.8	22.3	14.0	9.1	5.7

2. Fortress France

Immediately after the Gaullist landslide in the June 1968 parliamentary elections (following the virtual anarchy of the preceding month), the outgoing Prime Minister, Georges Pompidou, warned his countrymen that 'for over fifty years France's industries had been cosseted behind protective barriers' but that, with Europe's gradual integration, this age was over. Thus, the era of isolation was clearly delimited: it had begun with the First World War. Although the Méline tariff had been introduced in 1892 and duties were raised again in 1910, pre-1914 protectionism had remained moderate. It was geared mainly to protecting domestic farmers by warding off cheap agricultural imports in a bid to slow down much-feared structural change (in particular rural migration to the cities). Industry, by contrast, was left comparatively unprotected and this brand of protectionism was powerless to stop the pre-1914 trade boom from knocking at the country's door. We must therefore seek other reasons for France's shrinking market share of manufactures (see Table 3.3) and the rigidity of its comparative advantage structure until the 1960s.

Prewar protectionism, however, provided the 'paradigm' for interwar commercial policy. At the outbreak of the First World War, the tariff and currency convertibility were suspended and the northern continental border was closed by military operations, while the government was gradually taking over the management and allocation of foreign trade. This policy was finalised in March 1917 by the introduction of 'consortiums', made up of employers and civil servants, which controlled the import and export of a growing number of commodities. Rationing was introduced for necessities and the country came to depend heavily for supplies on its allies and colonies.

Despite promises of a return to 'normal' (i.e. prewar) conditions, the dismantling of government controls and intervention remained partial and precarious. The conflict had turned the country from a net creditor (the second largest in 1914) to net debtor vis-à-vis the rest of the world; it had accumulated enormous liabilities, both public and private, towards British and American financial institutions. For this reason, the trade balance and the balance of payments were henceforth to be of the utmost concern to the public authorities.

Throughout the 1920s French governments insisted that debt repayments should be linked to reparation payments by a defeated Germany. But prospects far exceeded capabilities and postponement, followed by partial default, soured French–American relations. It reinforced a feeling of isolation among the French and their conviction of having to rely on the country's 'own resources'. It gave 'national economics' a second and forceful breath of life.

During this period the resumption of normal trading conditions was preempted by the threat of a payments crisis and the instability of financial markets as the real cost of the war became finally apparent and inflation, once a slow creep, gradually accelerated. Trade, boosted by the immense needs of reconstruction, resumed unhampered by much-eroded (through inflation) tariff duties. Commercial legislation was revised in the general tariff of 1928 after the franc's first devaluation. Nevertheless the new peg at 20 per cent of the franc's prewar (gold) value sustained a spectacular revival of exports until their collapse in 1932. But subsequently, as the Depression spread like wildfire across the continent, the government took emergency measures in the hope of averting the kind of balance of payments crisis which was engulfing other countries. Customs duties were raised, quotas introduced (on 58 per cent of all merchandise imports by 1937) and 'import surtaxes' came in after the devaluation of sterling (September 1931) and of the dollar (March 1933). Until the withdrawal from the gold standard in September 1936, the overvalued franc bore the brunt of the shock:

French exports contracted by 65 per cent from their 1927 peak. This was catastrophic for manufactured goods: French exports fell from 11.2 per cent of world exports in 1929 to 5.8 per cent in 1937. The country's openness rate shrank accordingly from 14.4 per cent to 8.6 per cent.

For the next fifty years foreign trade as well as FDI flows were to be monitored by government and treated as another SEM (import/export) company because of the implications of the balance of payments for the stability of the currency. In 1939 strict exchange controls were re-introduced and remained in force until 1959 (when they were lifted for non-residents). They were to be reimposed in 1969 and 1982. Liberalisation crept in only gradually and suffered dramatic setbacks. In this respect, it would take twenty-five years for fully fledged liberalisation to take hold.

Paradoxically the period of the 'sheltered economy' (1945–85) was also one of profound imbalances. To most commentators, there was little else that governments could have done. Concern for the balance of payments did not prevent the recurrence of capital flight and the perpetuation of deep imbalances. On the eve of the Second World War, France's economic isolation was probably 'as profound as that of autarchic Nazi Germany' (Asselain 1984).

The deterioration of the international position of the French economy is best illustrated by the collapse of the currency (see Figure 2.1). The franc, first devalued in 1926–8, had lost 99 per cent of its original value after the postwar settlement (1949). Between 1926 and 1983, a staggering total of fourteen devaluations were carried out by successive governments; in Europe only the Italian lira can match such a continuous erosion of such proportions. Wars naturally had taken their toll: the cost of the First World War amounted to four years of national income, while German occupation between 1940 and 1944 bled the country of its gold reserves and encouraged the Vichy authorities to use and abuse the printing press. But fiscal mismanagement in the inter- and postwar years, when rival economic interests competed to extort pecuniary advantages from weak governments, also accounts for the currency's continuous depreciation. Inflation became a form of government policy which appeased competing claims and presented the enormous advantage of slowly but surely eroding the public debt.

3. The balance sheet of French colonialism

Colonisation constitutes the third pillar which, besides protectionism and 'national economics', epitomised France's posture vis-à-vis the rest of the world until the 1960s. Until recently there was little doubt among most observers (expert or lay) that French imperialism had been broadly beneficial to the home country. While its advocates celebrated the benefits France supposedly drew from her colonial empire in terms of scarce resources and trade, anti-imperialists denounced the oppression and exploitation of non-Europeans. The view that the empire contributed significantly to French economic development was long regarded as self-evident. However, this contention cannot stand up to close examination of the record: to the whole economy the gains from colonisation were scanty and/or short-lived.

Like most other European powers, France assembled the components of a 'second colonial empire'[2] in the thirty years after the Congress of Berlin in 1878. By 1913 it covered eleven million square kilometres and numbered a population of some fifty million people. The Versailles treaty of 1919 consolidated these possessions by granting France League of Nations mandates over former German and Ottoman colonies. Like its British counterpart, the French empire included possessions with varying legal status and ties to the home country. There were outright colonies subject to semi-military rule in Western and Equatorial Africa; protectorates in Tunisia, Morocco, Laos and Cambodia; and *départements** (in Algeria and the French West Indies) approaching the status enjoyed by British dominions.

Stagnant demography, the hostility of the natural environment, and the lack of obvious economic opportunities account for the fact that French emigration to the colonies remained a mere trickle. Prospective settlers were so scarce that the government at first used the colonies as 'dumping grounds' for assorted political prisoners and convicts (thus New Caledonia, Algeria and Devil's Island off the Guyana coast – Captain Dreyfus's prison). What little 'free' emigration did take place had to be subsidised by the government (notably emigration to Algeria). At the time of the 1931 Paris

---

[2] The 'first' had been gained (and lost) in the eighteenth century.

colonial exhibition – the zenith of French imperialism – only just over 3 per cent of the inhabitants of French overseas territories were of European stock. A mere 36,000 French people emigrated between the wars when, conversely, the country was absorbing two million foreign immigrants. Over the eighty years of its existence, the French empire served as little more than an exotic destination for holidaymakers and eccentrics – and as a 'rifle range' for the army.

In colonial propaganda – as in denunciations of imperialism – control over strategic or valuable raw materials was supposed to provide a substantial return on the necessarily expensive investment in colonial infrastructures. Again there is little evidence that this was the case: even if individual mining and trading companies did very well for a time at exploiting and transporting natural resources (minerals) and produce (wine and fruit), the cumulative and long-term effect was a total loss.

A conservative estimate puts 'direct' colonial expenditure by the government between 1894 and 1939 at nine billion francs, to which 'indirect' military expenditure of no less than five billion must be added. The arithmetic of capital flows is less straightforward. On one reckoning, cumulative private and public investment on the eve of the Second World War was some fifteen billion francs, two thirds of which came from the public purse.

Beyond the sometimes dramatic upswings of their stockmarket quotations, the profitability of colonial business ventures seems to have been, in the long term, illusory. Private investment represented only 10 per cent of French FDI prior to the first war; it recovered in the 1920s, but collapsed in the 1930s; it had to be constantly and increasingly propped up by public transfers and government guarantee. Only a handful of firms turned out to be sustainable and profitable businesses: the twenty largest colonial concerns earned 61 per cent of total profits in 1929 and 68 per cent in 1958. 'Geographically it was restricted to Algeria and Indochina' (Marseille 1984). Between 1945 and 1958, public loans came to represent 80 per cent of all capital inflows to the empire (by then renamed the 'French Union'). In addition, the government had to extend interest payment relief, subsidise loans and underwrite local infrastructure programmes as private investment dried up in the wake of growing social and political unrest. In the last decade of its existence, the 'Union' was draining substantial resources from the homeland, something that inevitably crippled domestic capital formation at home. Apart from generous social security payments to North Africa and other overseas territories, the structural deficit in the empire's trade balance came to be financed, directly or indirectly (because they shared a common currency), by French taxpayers. The realisation that the 'imperial connection was increasingly becoming a drain, not an asset' played a significant role in converting a majority of politicians and officials (as well as growing numbers of voters) to the idea of decolonisation and led some to denounce 'the illusion of the franc zone'.

By the 1950s it had become plain that empire trade was in fact contributing to France's balance of payments deficit, thereby deepening the 'dollar gap'. Empire trade, by providing a 'life-raft' to some failing industries at home and a 'safe haven' to others, was skewing French exports towards basic, run-of-the-mill necessities. Between the 1880s and the 1950s, the empire's growing share in total trade sustained the illusion that it was essential to the country's trade balance. The gains were in fact scanty because the economy at large would have benefited from competing on third-country markets, and the manufactured goods exported to colonial markets were largely purchased by French settlers, most of whom – such as civil servants and the military – drew a livelihood from the homeland. Likewise, imports from the empire could in theory relieve pressure on the balance of payments, but if subsidised directly or indirectly (via subsidies to merchant shipping), they were in fact more expensive than comparable goods from outside. Together, imports and exports pushed up prices and production costs and only offered the French economy 'an opportunity to remain backward'.

However, France's colonial experiment cannot be appraised only through economic facts and realities. In both world wars the empire supplied a sizeable contingent of servicemen – some of whom ultimately gave their lives – and in the second it supplied a base for the Free French and (in North Africa) a jumping-off point for the Anglo-American landing in southern Italy. Multifaceted cultural and emotional ties bound France to her formerly subject populations overseas. However, as soon as politicians came to realise that the empire was a hopelessly loss-making venture diverting much-needed resources (economic, human and military) from domestic development, its fate was sealed. The French left Indochina in 1954; that same year Morocco and Tunisia gained independence. Algeria had to wait until 1962. In the meantime all of France's 'black African' territories became independent. Today, France retains only three overseas *départements** (Guadeloupe, Martinique and Réunion) and four territories in the Pacific – all an integral part of the EU. That is all she can afford.

4. Towards a 'new age'?

Concomitant with decolonisation, the advent of the Fifth Republic in 1958 represented a major watershed, not only in political and institutional terms but also in so far as it set the stage for subsequent developments in foreign and commercial policy. The turn of the 1960s marked France's major reversal of attitude towards the rest of the world. After short-lived attempts between 1949 and 1952, the Fourth Republic had made little headway on commitments made at Bretton Woods (1944) to GATT, the OEEC and the WPU (all created in 1948) to open borders to foreign trade and investment and reinstate the franc's convertibility. Two decisive factors set France on the path of liberalisation: De Gaulle's commitment to pursue European integration, and the monetary reform after the currency stabilisation of 1959, indispensable after the humiliating rescue by the IMF in 1957. This enabled France to comply with recommendations in the Treaty of Rome (1957), banning import quotas and lowering tariff duties by 10 per cent in 1958 and 40 per cent by 1962. On 1 July 1968 the EEC became a full customs union with complete free trade between EEC member states, which quickly became each other's major trade partners. Similarly the external tariff was aligned on the lowest rate among member countries. It was subsequently lowered following the GATT negotiations of the Kennedy (1963) and subsequent Tokyo (1973) and Uruguay (1986) rounds.

A substantial acceleration of foreign trade ensued: surpassing annual growth rates of 6.5 per cent in the 1950s, French trade grew at a rate of 10.8 per cent per annum between 1959 and 1974; the increase fell to 6 per cent during the oil crisis years but resumed a healthy pace in the 1980s. This expansion brought with it greater diversification and a growing contribution of services and 'invisibles' to the country's current account. France regained the fourth rank it had held in the past among world exporters. Its openness rate, 12 per cent in 1959 – barely above that of 1949 (10.8 per cent) – leapt to 20.7 per cent in 1979 and 28.7 per cent in 1999. Import penetration followed the same course, especially for a wide range of semi-durable goods.

At the same time there occurred a dramatic shift among France's trading partners from the franc zone* (created in 1946 with its colonial empire) to EEC member states. The share of the franc zone (until then France's major partner) was 21 per cent in 1956 but fell to 4 per cent in 1970, swapping position with the Federal Republic of Germany. Over the period, trade with other advanced economies, among them EEC (now EU) partners, has taken the lion's share of French trade.

By and large, and despite repeated temporary setbacks (the 1967 recession, the two 1970s oil crises, the Socialists' first term from 1981 to 1984), the balance of payments improved in the long run. After a period of 'structural deficit' between 1974 and 1990 (due in part to the country's heavy energy bill), trade experienced a revival in the 1990s thanks to deflation and the euro's[3] *de facto* devaluation of 25 per cent. Meanwhile, the country was recording growing surpluses on its invisibles balance.

With hindsight, such a transformation seems indeed dramatic, but to a large extent France has trodden the same path as other Western nations. This transition happened, moreover, in a framework (set up in the immediate postwar period) of relatively close supervision of trade and investment by government authorities: BFCE and COFACE (created in 1944 and 1945 respectively) were entrusted with settling outstanding balances, insuring freight and protecting the assets of export/import dealers. They continued to exercise these and other ancillary functions such as the prospecting of foreign markets. Government guidance was undoubtedly necessary at the time of reconstruction and the Marshall Plan, and it helped strengthen positions and reduce risks in the age of the 'closed economy'; but, heavily biased as it was towards large public procurement contracts, it is likely that the kind of marketing fostered by centralised and

---

[3] The ECU was the euro's predecessor, introduced in 1979 as the common reserve currency of the European Monetary System. The beginning of the 25 per cent devaluation goes back to the ECU period.

Table 3.4 Share of French trade with present EU member countries (%)

EU 15	1913	1938	1958	1996
Exports	59.1	41.7	32.5	62.9
Imports	42.8	33.1	30.5	63.0
Coverage*	113	84	97	104

* 100: trade balance in equilibrium.

bureaucratic procedures might be inadequate in a rapidly changing economic environment.

All the evidence points to the fact that 'growing exposure to competitive world markets through international trade and investment stimulate[d French] growth and structural change' (Adams, 1989: 205). At the same time, over the long run, France's position seems to have been remarkably resilient: in 2000 it held the same rank (fourth) among world traders as it did in 1900, and today as yesterday its main partners are still essentially found among Western advanced economies, mostly its immediate neighbours (see Table 3.4). Its present specialisation range also recalls traditional French products already known and sought after in 1914 or 1939: alcoholic drinks (such as wines and spirits), perfumes and toiletries, cereals, vehicle parts and pharmaceuticals. In the past forty years, however, France has had to shed, under the pressure of competition, a number of former foreign exchange earners such as fine clothing, shoes and leather and petroleum products. Indisputable advantages have been acquired in services (finance, transport and maintenance and, last but not least, tourism). But in commodity trade, the country's specialisation in semi-processed and manufactured goods, remarkably similar in a sense to that of the USA, exhibits signs of weakness (see Table 3.5). It is excessively segmented by 'stage' of product rather than by 'stream' (or range of associated products). Besides, French competitiveness, as evidenced by comparative advantage indicators, appears weaker than that of other comparable countries.

To conclude, France's present position vis-à-vis the rest of the world resembles that at the beginning of the twentieth century in so far as she is still a net exporter of capital – though to a lesser extent

Table 3.5 Outstanding moves in comparative advantage, 1967–97

Specialisation	Positive	Negative
Reversed	tourism	leather and shoes
	services	clothing
	electricity	natural gas
	electronic components	oil by-products
Reduced	farm produce	personal vehicles
	domestic appliances	electrical goods
	meat and fish	shipping
	machinery	metal manufactures
Stable		tyres
		cement
		armaments
		coke
Strengthened	aerospace	computer equipment
	drink	plastics
	perfumes and toiletries	processed tobacco
	cereals	agricultural equipment

than formerly (French FDI represents only 5 per cent of GNP – half its pre-1914 level). Although France also attracts substantial foreign investment (witness its 900-plus McDonald's outlets), there is evidence that French capital is finding more promising opportunities to grow and bear fruit abroad rather than at home. French companies control 19,000 subsidiaries worldwide with 3.5 million employees – who could, in the opinion of some observers, be more profitably occupied at home.

Chapter 4
The changing face of Colbertism

It is a deeply ingrained belief among French experts and in public opinion at large that France possesses specific and superior political arrangements and that they are in any case best suited to the French character and *Weltanschauung*. This exception assigns a preeminent role to the state in directing economic life, expressed in the term *dirigisme* or *volontarisme*. A forceful tradition among the political elite, it is alleged to have been inspired by Jean-Baptiste Colbert (1619–83), minister to Louis XIV. In the golden age of mercantilism, Colbert conceived the country's material wellbeing as subservient to its politics and the grandeur of the king and the state.[1] His ambition was for the state to brace its energies to this end, to build up the country's defence, to promote self-sufficiency and to pursue full employment, while maintaining standards of fairness and morality in the marketplace. He advocated government control of the balance of payments, but also direct intervention in economic life, and introduced extensive regulation in the labour and commodity markets with a view to promoting national champions and strategic industries. Colbert's ideas have left deep marks in the French psyche: the state embodies the common good, the organising force of society. Colbert's principles have largely inspired French government intervention throughout the twentieth century. How these authoritarian strands were integrated with the modern French republican tradition requires some preliminary explanation.

[1] While Colbert bequeathed his name to French government intervention, Colbert's protagonists (the representatives of the business community he had summoned to hear their demands) unknowingly coined the term for the 'hands-off' brand of economic policy (as extolled later by the classical economists) as they responded 'Laissez-nous faire' (Leave it to us).

1. Ways and means in the republican state

1.1 Republican ideology and the egalitarian ideal

In the French psyche the country's form of government represents an intrinsically different (and sometimes superior) form of democracy. The republican *Etat* or state (one of the few French words to take a capital) is not perceived as a mere administrative apparatus providing a number of services to the voting and taxpaying public: it is the highest expression of the nation's collective will and rationality. Historians concur: the state through the ages has been the organising force of French society and in the twentieth century 'the instrument of political emancipation and economic rationalization' (Rosanvallon, 1990). While individual politicians can be corrupt and/or incompetent, the state never ceases to guide the nation's destiny and take responsibility for its prosperity and power: it is the bulwark of the French way of life. As a result, the majority of scholarly accounts of postwar French economic development sometimes read as a saga of enlightened officials driving the unthinking and industrious masses towards the safety of a peaceful/glorious/affluent future. It is unclear how the political elite should be expected to forsake personal advantage and serve the public good. Some commentators, influenced by constitutionalists, assume that the French government machinery is so conceived as to ensure the pursuit of this goal. But statist ideology more obviously rests on a different set of values and convictions. The first has to do with a belief in the intrinsic moral superiority of politics over economics (a characteristic legacy of aristocratic societies) along with a deep distrust of 'unchecked' market forces. Hence the greater emphasis placed on equality as against liberty: because economic relationships are always supposed to entail some form of exploitation, it is left to the state to redress the balance and guarantee some measure of fairness. In this sense the French see their republican democracy as superior to the Anglo-Saxon (read American) variety.

1.2 France's biggest undertaking

Exhaustive information on French government employment is difficult to pin down. This may be an unforeseen outcome of the expansion of the nation-state in the twentieth century. However, French

Table 4.1 Size of the civil service and its share in total employment

Year	Central government (thsds)	Local authorities (thsds)	Total (thsds)	Percentage
1914	640	250	785	3.9
1921	795	290	1085	5.5
1936	982	330	1312	7.2
1947	1055	545	1600	8.4
1962	2066	694	2760	14.0
1978	2677	1311	3988	18.5
1990	3058	2148	5206	23.1
2000	3258	2362	5620	24.7

public administration, or the public sector as a whole, whether or not local authorities are included, has remained the country's main employer throughout the century. Before the First World War the share of public employment in France was already among the highest by international standards (6 per cent compared to a European average of 4 to 5 per cent). In 2000 one of every four workers was in public employment.

More than the aggregate numbers, it is the centralisation of France's state apparatus (reflecting the concentration of political power) which stands out as its major distinguishing feature – a legacy of the Ancien Régime and the Napoleonic era. The central organs of the French state, all located in the capital, Paris, control the scattered provincial outposts and manage them from the top. As a result, the balance of means has always been tipped towards central government and local authorities have always accounted for a relatively smaller share of public employment (between 15 and 20 per cent of the total) than in comparable European states. This does not in fact do justice to the actual situation, as the salaries of some categories of local government employees come out of the government's budget.

Already by 1914, public employment was not limited to the civil service: public administration – the *fonction publique** – included a variety of agencies providing non-traded and sometimes indivisible services as well as several extensions in the traded goods sector. In addition to civil administrators, judges and policemen, postmen (since 1850), teachers (since 1881) and a numerous army of tax-collectors, the state supported from its annual budget an assortment of railwaymen, industrial workers, gamekeepers, supervisors, stewards and overseers in small but burgeoning public corporations. The nineteenth-century notion of a minimal 'nightwatchman state' (concentrating on key missions of law and order) had expanded to include tasks of market regulation such as sustaining employment. Despite the diversity of jobs, positions and working conditions, all state employees enjoyed certain common advantages which consolidated into the 'Civil Service Statute' passed by Parliament in 1946.

Until the Second World War, as overall civilian employment was contracting, the relative size of the public sector doubled from 8 to 15 per cent of total employment. This increase proceeded by successive jolts, through the extension of already-existing services in the wake of interwar reconstruction. In its aftermath, public sector job creation accelerated. While the baby boom resulted in a 46 per cent increase in the working population between 1954 and 1990, public employment almost doubled during the same period.[2]

Adolf Wagner had predicted back in the 1880s that more prosperous societies were bound to expand collective and social services which fell within the purview of national governments. Contemporaries observed, and historians confirm, that under the postwar social settlement the expansion of the public sector was continuous, as if there existed a 'ratchet mechanism' (Delorme and André, 1981) which prevented public employment (as well as public expenditure), from sliding back to previous lower levels.

This seemingly unchecked rise was partly due, on the demand side, to the unabated attractiveness of careers in public services and hence to cultural preferences, but also, on the supply side, to the growing complexity of a government apparatus over which ministers and Parliament gradually lost control. Hiring procedures, in particular, have become so impenetrable that by a civil service minister's own admission, no one knows exactly how many people are paid from the public purse. Thus 'safe job creation' dynamics seem to have played a disproportionate role in the extension of the French public service. By European standards France has today

---

[2] The figures just quoted do not cover the payrolls of public corporations.

Table 4.2 Public expenditure as a proportion of GDP (%)

	1913	1950	1973	1998
France	14.5	23.2	37.6	52.4
Germany	17.0	32.4	30.4	47.6
United Kingdom	11.8	28.8	34.2	39.7
USA	8.0	19.8	21.4	30.1

one of the highest proportion of public workers, close to 29 per cent of total employment including public corporations (this compares with rates of under 20 per cent for most Western countries).[3] If the 1.5 million civil service pensioners are added, they constitute together a numerous, well-organised constituency of over eight million people which politicians are naturally wary of antagonizing.

1.3 Government finance: income and expenditure

In so far as the lion's share of state expenditure consists of public servants' wages, there is an obvious link between the size of the public sector and its financial resources. These expanded in the course of the twentieth century by a factor of thirty, whereas GNP grew only by a factor of eight (see Table 4.2).

From the beginning, France found itself 'leading the pack' among the 'big spenders' in Europe. Before the First World War the public debt approximated to one full year of GNP. Subsequently, the government had to shoulder the burden of a destructive war and reconstruction – and twenty years later of yet another invasion and occupation – with an obsolete taxation system originally laid out during the French Revolution. During the first war the Clemenceau government upgraded the tax yield by introducing income tax (originally passed in July 1914, introduced in 1917) followed by a turnover tax in 1919 (as well as a short-lived tax on 'abnormal wartime profits'). What gave interwar governments a little more leeway after Poincaré's stabilisation of the franc in 1926

---

[3] At the zenith of Socialism, public employment in Britain reached 6.3 million in 1968 (including 2 million employees of public corporations) representing 24 per cent of total employment.

was the multiplication and extension of a variety of sales and transaction taxes. Despite these increments, the government's resources always proved inadequate to its ambitions, as the persistence and size of the budget deficit shows (see Figure 4.1). The inadequacy of tax levies could be offset only by a constantly swelling debt mitigated by a steady rate of inflation.

Only after the Second World War did the French government acquire the means to match resources to expenditure. The income tax base was greatly extended, progressivity was introduced in the income tax schedules and, in 1954, a catch-all TVA (or VAT) on all kinds of transactions was brought in to replace the myriad of *centimes additionnels* (supertaxes). Over the years VAT which, in 1998, has come to provide 48 per cent of all government revenue, has proved to be the government's politically safest and economically most reliable tax. Both VAT and the array of social security contributions have helped to ensure a stable and reliable source of revenue for twenty years. The oil crisis unsettled the balance once again. Between 1975 and 1982 several measures were taken to shift the burden of fuel price increases on to corporations. Such was the 'business tax' introduced in 1976 and the IGF, a wealth tax, in 1982.

By the end of the century, France's tax system was tending to converge towards a broad Western European model: it now relies heavily on consumption, and bears proportionately more on labour than on capital income[4] (marginal rates of corporate taxation fell from 65 per cent to 33 per cent between 1982 and 1995) and more on personal than on corporate wealth.[5]

Public spending has been the driving force behind the spectacular rise in public revenue. The pattern was set during the First World War, as urgent need required governments to make immediate commitments to scale up the war effort. The Depression of the 1930s reinforced this trend, although deflationary policies in the early 1930s aimed at (but scarcely achieved) the stabilisation of public spending (Figure 4.1). The Second World War continued

---

[4] A consequence of the overwhelming share (90 per cent) of labour in total income.
[5] Recently, left-wing and right-wing governments alike have attempted – so far unsuccessfully – to increase the income from taxation by reforming the ponderous tax bureaucracy, still traditionally split between tax assessment and tax collection.

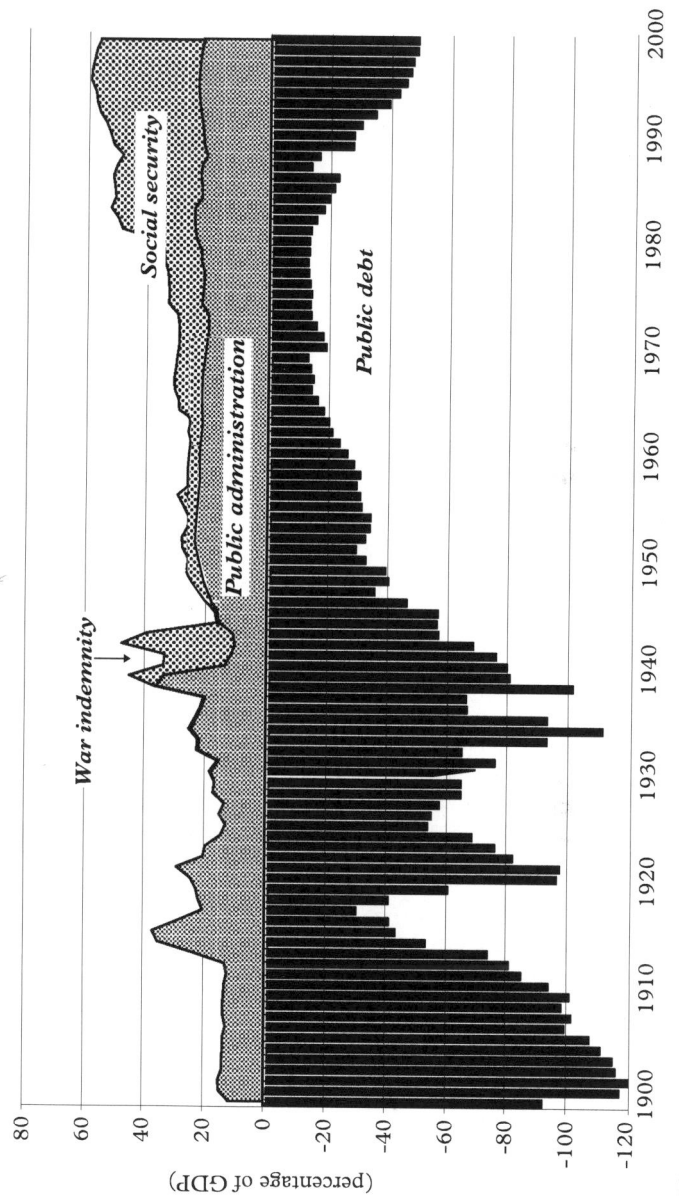

Figure 4.1 Share of public spending and the public debt in GDP, 1900–2000

this trend. The traditional interpretation is that the dramatic expansion and diversification of public expenditure was the outcome of a sequence of 'extraordinary' circumstances: war, reconstruction, depression, war, occupation, reconstruction. Another more heterodox view emphasises the enduring contradiction, endemic in parliamentary regimes, between the electorate's willingness to spend and reluctance to pay, and on the part of the political authorities, an inability to find any solution to this persistent problem.

Public expenditure in peacetime escalated from around 12 per cent of GDP in 1900 to over 20 per cent in the interwar period, progressively rising to 30 per cent from the 1960s and 40 per cent in the 1980s. In the last decade of the century public expenditure (including government spending and social security payments) has hovered around and above 50 per cent of GDP. Postwar trends were common to the developed world as demand for the provision of collective services (including health, education and transport) increased with rising living standards. Social welfare payments and the upkeep of the welfare state have accounted for the maintenance of high levels of public spending after the urgent needs of war and reconstruction.

2. From market supervision to market control

A distinction is generally made between the relatively laissez-faire policies before the Second World War and postwar extensive interventionism. However, by the turn of the twentieth century the French state had already ceased to play the role of 'nightwatchman' and was exercising considerable leverage on the economy. In that sense, the 'great transformation' identified by Polanyi (1944), by which nineteenth-century governments loosened controls over market activities, had only been partially applied in France. Leading economist Paul Leroy-Beaulieu (1843–1916) coined the term 'propellant conservatism' to describe the Third Republic's attitude towards the economy.

2.1 Market organisation and supervision

Under the parliamentary regime established by the constitution of the Third Republic (1875), the executive was put under the strict control of the legislature. Government policy, the necessary compromise between shifting majorities and conflicting interests, typically sought to strike a balance between 'proactive' strategies intended to foster modernisation and 'reactive' tactics to extend assistance to hard-pressed groups and promote equal opportunities. Consequently, most twentieth-century governments have consistently tried to distort market mechanisms and restrict competition in one way or another. Only recently, under the impulse of EU directives, has progress been made towards improving market efficiency. Before that, one continuous line of action has been the creation of 'niches' sheltered from market pressures – foreign or domestic. Corporatism, the segmentation of professional activities, in theory the official economic policy of the Vichy regime, in practice ruled large swathes of the pre-1940 (and indeed post-1945) domestic economy.

Here again signs of schizophrenia are evident. Freedom of enterprise (including a ban on discrimination in employment) figured prominently among basic civil rights guaranteed by the constitution(s),[6] and was imbedded in case law upheld by the Conseil d'Etat, France's highest court.[7] But the trend in economic policy, reinforced by wartime controls, has been away from an economic system shaped by individual initative towards growing preemptive control of employment opportunities. Until the 1960s, the government systematically favoured the segmentation of markets and the preservation of special status prevalent in services which were largely insulated from foreign competition. This applied to transport (air, road, sea and rail), banking, medical and legal services, and retail trade. In retailing, legislation was systematically skewed to prop up small retailers vis-à-vis chain or department stores (loi Le Pallen, 1928; loi Royer, 1973). In the 1960s, the struggles of Leclerc to build itself up from a co-operative store in Landernau (Brittany) in 1949 to a major supermarket chain, in the face of fierce resistance from competitors, illustrates the ambivalence of state authorities towards fully fledged competition. The loi Royer of 1973 subjected the opening of new supermarkets to drastic rules

---

[6] Successive constitutions date from 1875, 1946 and 1958. The Universal Declaration of the Rights of Man served as a preamble to the constitutions of the Fourth and Fifth Republics.
[7] *Conseils des prud'hommes** (industrial tribunals) were created in 1848.

and the supervision of ad hoc committees. Such restrictions (or *numerus clausus*) also applied to a variety of other activities, from pharmacies and public notaries to driving schools and locksmiths.

The regulation of the labour market constitutes a major area of twentieth-century government intervention, but attention has essentially focused on the effects it has had on the living and working conditions of workers in industry. Rather than promoting efficient channels of collective bargaining between employers and employees, the state has sought to manage industrial relations directly. Several factors may have motivated this enduring option, including the threat of industrial action to public order, the state's 'philanthropic mission', the existence of a substantial state sector and the outstanding fact that settlements were agreed on the condition that the Treasury would make up any unaccounted-for benefit to the claimants. To the political right, government intervention promised an end to the class struggle, and to the left the guarantee of fair treatment for their 'natural' constituents. This arrangement, formalised in the postwar period under the name of *paritarisme*,* set up decision-making bodies at different levels made up of union, employers' and government representatives.[8] As a result, major improvements in workers' welfare have generally been shaped and sanctioned by parliamentary legislation on the 'one size fits all' principle (rather than being the outcome of bi-partisan agreement). Working time and working conditions in industry were successively shaped by the prohibition of Sunday trading (1906), the introduction of the mandatory limitation on the working week (1919) and of paid holidays (1936), mandatory retirement at 60 (1981), the establishment of collective work contracts (1936), works councils (1946), the minimum wage (1950) and the sliding scale (1968). The posture of the French state as the guarantor of the public good has made it the ubiquitous regulator of industrial conflicts.

2.2 Currency and financial management

Even before the advent of outright 'demand management' in the 1950s, the French government and its Treasury exercised

---

[8] Still in force today in the public service and in large concerns (over 500 employees). Union representation is limited to the five 'representative' unions as defined in the immediate postwar period.

considerable leverage over money creation and financial circuits. The institution responsible for the money supply, the Banque de France (originally set up as a private institution in 1800 with a monopoly on banknote issue since 1848), suffered few encroachments and was in great part responsible for monetary stability before the First World War. The bank gradually lost its independence during that war and in the interwar period as it was repeatedly required by the Treasury to provide advances to ease the government's cashflow. In 1936, the Popular Front government placed it *de facto* under Treasury supervision, its twenty-member board being henceforth appointed by the government. Fully fledged nationalisation followed in 1945.[9] The government's hold on the money supply had in the meantime been enhanced by the priority granted to numerous government bond issues. In addition, the state increased its stake in the financial system by spawning several credit institutions. Pre-1914 forerunners included the Caisse des Dépôts et Consignations (created in 1816) and two networks of provincial banks: the Crédit Agricole and the Caisses d'Epargne (both savings banks). The Banque Populaire and Crédit National were added in 1917 and 1919 respectively. By 1938, two thirds of all bank deposits were in public or quasi-public institutions which together supplied 40 per cent of all investment by private firms (Gueslin, 1994). But the government's hold over the banking system, justified at first by the necessities of reconstruction, subsequently tended to crowd out productive investment. The state's influence did not stop there, however. Of an estimated total of 150 billion francs, 77 per cent of the cost of the First World War was financed by borrowing (and only 16 per cent by taxation); the debt accumulated was so huge that it was virtually impossible for the government to repay it. The use and abuse of the printing press necessarily generated massive currency depreciation. As a result, the French inflation record in the twentieth century is one of the worst in Europe: prices multiplied by a factor of seven between 1914 and 1938, by a factor of nineteen between 1938 and 1949, and again by eleven between 1950 and 1990.

---

[9] Before the creation of the ECB, the central bank's independence was restored to satisfy Maastricht Treaty guidelines in 1993.

Table 4.3 Devaluations of the franc, 1928–58

Dates	Finance minister	Magnitude (per cent)	Equivalent (gold mg)	Exchange rate FF to $	FF to £
1876–1914		100	327.5	5.18	25.25
June 1926	Poincaré	80	65.5	25.42	124.04
Oct. 1936	Auriol	25	49.0	25.14	124.42
Nov. 1938	Reynaud	44	27.5	37.85	176.78
Nov. 1944		–	–	49.62	200
Dec. 1945	Pleven	70	8.29	119.10	480
Jan. 1948	Mayer	50	4.212	214.39	865
Oct. 1948	Queuille	20	3.372	264	1062
Oct. 1949	Petsche	24.5	2.545	350	980
June 1958	Gaillard	7.7	2.35	420	1176
Dec. 1958	Pinay-Rueff	15	2.0	493.70	1382

By the mid-century, after a string of devaluations, the franc (whose free convertibility was briefly reinstated between 1928 and 1938) had lost 99 per cent of its pre-1914 value. Political decision-makers wavered between impotence and schizophrenia, calling for 'defence of the franc' policies while implementing inflationary policies followed by devaluations (as Figure 4.1 shows, deflationary or 'stabilisation' policies were extremely timid and short-lived).[10]

Although the two world wars took their toll,[11] the collapse of the currency appears as the result of fiscal mismanagement in periods of peace. This mismanagement was responsible for the annihilation of the vast quantity of savings accumulated since the end of the nineteenth century – roughly equivalent to 45 billion gold francs (or one third of the pre-1914 national wealth) without taking capital flight into account. In view of the comparative performance of the French economy in the first half of the century,[12] serious doubt can be cast on the efficacy of the complex of policies which led to such

[10] Between 1914 and 1950 the government budget was in surplus in only four fiscal years.
[11] Mandatory payments to the German occupying forces amounted to between 19.3 and 36.6 per cent of national income annually between 1940 and 1944.
[12] In 1938 GDP was only 20 per cent higher than in 1913 (and 34.5 per cent higher in 1949), putting France at the bottom of the league of Western European economies.

destruction and helped to lastingly isolate France from the rest of the world.[13]

2.3 'State socialism' or 'State capitalism'?

Outside fiscal policies and money management with obvious macroeconomic implications, government intervention moved in several directions under the Third Republic. Politically, the period (especially after 1902) was dominated by the centre-left 'Radicals'[14] who appealed to the median voters ('les petits') whom they pledged to protect against 'les gros' (the fat cats). Having lost their working-class voters to the Socialist and, after 1920, Communist parties,[15] the Radicals supported the preservation of the status quo, a position which entailed promoting of policies aimed at sheltering certain activities and relieving specific constituencies.

Trade protectionism was the main policy instrument used to seal off traditional industries (including agriculture) from foreign competition. First brought in at the end of the nineteenth century (the Méline tariff of 1892), intricate trade restrictions and controls kept production costs relatively high but managed to slow down 'structural change'. The external tariff was complemented by internal duties on the domestic transport of goods and statutory restrictions on services. Suspended in 1914 and eroded by postwar inflation, the prewar tariff, officially reinstated in 1921, was finally revised in 1928. In the interval, relative free trade had positive spillovers for reconstruction. At the onset of the Depression, however, trade barriers were raised again to unprecedented heights: by 1933 most traded goods were subject to import controls or quotas. This policy contributed to the collapse of French trade and helped prolong the Depression until 1939. Designed originally to protect small-scale farming and traditional industries, protectionism in a context of monetary uncertainties became a tool to supplement monetary policy in so far as it allowed control over the balance of trade, and

---

[13] Convertibility of the franc, suspended in 1939, was not reinstated until 1958, only to be suspended again in 1969. Exchange controls were finally removed in 1986.
[14] The 'radical party' was founded in 1901; its full name was the 'Radical and Radical-socialist Party'.
[15] When the French Section of the Communist International (SFIC) split from the old Socialist party (SFIO).

hence the balance of payments. For the same reasons protectionism was revived strongly in the 1950s until European integration and international co-operation (under the GATT rounds) forced its gradual unravelling.

The second set of policies with conspicuous distorting effects aimed at promoting certain sectors by means of grants and subsidies. Before the First World War only a handful of industries benefited from government largesse: flax and beet growers and shipbuilders were outstanding examples. Given budgetary constraints it could only be extended to relatively small constituencies. More ambitious were the public works programmes launched at regular intervals in times of depression. Usually named after their promoters (Baudin 1903, Tardieu 1929, Steeg-Laval 1931, Marquet 1934, Bedouce 1936 and Reynaud 1938), they aimed at stimulating product demand for ailing industries (typically construction, engineering and transport) by financing infrastructure projects (railway lines, ports, highways and public utility networks). This type of intervention further supplemented a burgeoning public sector. In 1914 it comprised an assortment of small-scale industries (sixty-four in total), including the tobacco and match monopoly, tapestry, furniture, porcelain manufacture and horse-breeding; it grew by leaps and bounds after the First World War.

Both historical and ideological causes explain the extension of government ownership and control in allegedly 'strategic' industries during the interwar period. The notion of a 'public service' providing universal access *and* managed by the state was first championed by the Socialists and then endorsed by virtually all political parties. In rail transport, reconstruction in the 1920s brought railway companies a huge access of public funds in the form of remuneration and subsidies. In a context of emergent overcapacity, the government countered by imposing strict guidelines, intervening to promote economies and impose caps on fares as well as freight charges. In 1937, the five existing operators were merged into a single public operator, the SNCF. In civil aviation, both supply (aircraft procurement) and demand (mail delivery) impelled government action towards the creation of Air France in 1933. In maritime transport, economic and social concerns also prompted the government to move into the management of shipyards and shipping companies. The SEM (mixed company) was the favoured solution adopted to effect this transfer: the government's 'golden share' ensured it retained control over policy. Outside the merchant navy (Compagnie Générale Transatlantique in 1931; SNCM from 1937), acquisitions were made in the nitrogen and potash industry (1921 and 1926), electricity in 1935 (production and distribution), petroleum in 1924 (Compagnie Française des Pétroles) and mining. With the creation of the ONIB (the wheat marketing board) in 1936 the government acquired wide influence over the pricing of agricultural produce. In communications, the telephone service, which had been a government monopoly since 1889, displayed a particularly pitiful performance. On the eve of the Second World War France had one of the smallest, most expensive[16] and least automated networks in Western Europe.

3. Big Brother's new tasks: economic management and social welfare

After the extensive tax reform of 1948 and the massive transfers under the Marshall Plan (representing 25 per cent of government revenue over four years), the state dramatically increased its leverage on the national economy, thereby fulfilling the aim of the 1930s, to 'obtain for the government the means to control the national economy' (M Debré).[17] By and large the 'socialisation' of the GNP broadly corresponded to the shift in people's preferences away from private consumption towards social or collective goods such as health and education.

Accordingly, most French historians are quick to adopt the distinction drawn by the 'Regulation school', between 'indirect regulation' by prewar laissez-faire governments using market mechanisms and the type which developed after the war whereby governments acquired the macroeconomic instruments required to steer the economy towards politically agreed goals. Consequently, the experience of *dirigisme** has been generally viewed favourably by historians who have been quick to attribute the successes of the 'Golden Age' to the large-scale substitution of public for private

---

[16] The managers of Ericsson's French subsidiary (which enjoyed a monopoly over the supply of handsets) used to refer to France as 'the golden cage'.
[17] Michel Debré (1912–96), the first Prime Minister of the Fifth Republic (1958–62) and the main author of the 1958 constitution.

decision-making. But to a large extent postwar interventionism exhibits a difference of scale, not of nature, with its predecessor, and no global counterfactual is yet available to test the validity of the second proposition.

3.1 Planning for a more secure future

The period of postwar reconstruction up to 1950 fostered the creation of institutions and policies designed to put macroeconomic levers under the control of central government. In the ideological climate of the time, in which Socialism loomed large on the horizon, this option was approved by a broad consensus of public opinion, which supported the view that capitalism had 'failed' and the Depression of the 1930s had proved positively that markets could not be left to automatically compensate for temporary setbacks. The main objectives were outlined in the CNR's 1943 programme, which called for vast 'structural' reforms along the lines of Socialist and Communist wartime manifestos (Andrieu, 1984). Inspired by the Soviet command economy (and to a lesser extent by Roosevelt's New Deal),[18] the postwar reforms also built on the initiatives of wartime Vichy officials such as the multiplication of marketing boards ('comités d'organisation') and the creation of equipment and telecommunications directorates (DGE and DGT).

The creation in 1946 of a central planning agency (CGP), the brainchild of its first head, Jean Monnet (1888–1979), has received considerable attention and is generally credited with successfully pulling the French economy out of the postwar quagmire and setting it on a growth path in the 1950s and 60s. The *Plans* set priorities in terms of output and employment, made investment recommendations, sought to co-ordinate policy objectives and advised the government on how best to attain them; the final decision, however, always rested with the Treasury (Margairaz, 1991). Credited with having 'consistently reduced business uncertainty' in the 1950s and 1960s (Carré *et al.*, 1975), the *Plan* was *de facto* set aside in the aftermath of the first oil crisis in 1973. The CGP has since served mainly as a government think tank. A number of additional agencies

---

[18] It is doubtful whether many French economists, let alone politicians, were familiar with the insights and policy recommendations of Keynes's *General Theory* (first published in French in 1942).

were created in its wake. The statistical office was reorganised and expanded under a new name, INSEE. The SEEF, also a Vichy creation, served as the main advisory body to the Treasury and laid the foundations of the French national accounts. The FME, originally set up to apportion Marshall Aid, became under a new name, FDES (1955), the main purveyor of financial assistance to industry in the 1950s. In 1963, another body, DATAR was created to tackle problems of urban congestion and remedy the widening gap between urban concentration and provincial 'desertification'. Central planning, designed to rebuild the country's infrastructures after the war, proved successful in boosting the production of indivisible (capital) goods, but a clumsy instrument when it came to anticipating and organising the production and distribution of consumer goods and semi-durables.

3.2 'Stop-and-go, French style'

Demand management was made possible by the greatly expanding resources at the disposal of the government. These included the use of the budget to tame the business cycle (the 'fine-tuning' of the economy), the control over the banking system and important stakes in the production system. To a large extent it was the insulation of the domestic economy which ensured the (temporary) success of macroeconomic policy in the 1950s and 1960s between recurrent devaluations (1949, 1959, 1969). These were signs that the erosion of the currency was a price the government was ready to pay for demand management. In 1957, as in 1963 and 1968, 'overheating' of the economy induced the government to use 'automatic stabilisers'. In the wake of the oil crisis, however, Keynesian policy instruments proved increasingly ill-adapted to cope with stagflation, and both the (boosting) *plans de relance** and (cooling) *plans de rigueur** were powerless to stem the spread of depression. After the slowdown set in, 'pump priming' was unable to reverse mounting unemployment or inflation. Such a strategy was last attempted in 1981–82 but had to be abruptly discarded, with a return to financial orthodoxy and three consecutive 'monetary readjustments'; it worsened, rather than improving, economic conditions at the time. Despite occasional bouts of financial largesse, the French government spurred by the demands of European integration, has since had to eschew macroeconomic policies of this type.

Table 4.4 Stop-and-go, French style: expansionary cycles (trough to trough)

Cycles	Government	Key figures	External constraints	Main policy instruments	Outcome
1949–53	centre-right	A. Pinay, J. Monnet	War in Indochina	budget deficit planning	price freeze (1952)
1953–7	centre-left	P. Mendès France, E. Faure	War in Algeria	public investment	devaluation (1958)
1957–9	left	F. Gaillard, A. Pinay		credit and wage controls	devaluation (1959)
1959–63	Gaullist	J. Rueff M. Debré	European integration	market liberalisation public investment	stabilisation plan
1963–8	Gaullist	Giscard d'Estaing			devaluation (1969)
1968–73	Gaullist		collapse of fixed parity	social transfers	oil crisis

3.3   The 'social state'

The creation of the postwar welfare state, and the redistribution of income it induced, contributed to reinforcing the 'economic stabilisers' which in turn consolidated the self-sustaining pattern of prosperity of the 'Golden Age'. Originally conceived on the basis of the prudential principle of personal insurance, its conception shifted in the 1970s to the universal, non-discriminatory provision of social services to all (and safety nets to outsiders). Its coverage likewise expanded from non-agricultural wage-earners to include the self-employed as well as members of the professions. Although signs of weakness were perceptible from the late 1960s, since the 1980s its sustainability has been threatened by an ageing population, high unemployment and the influx of low-skilled immigrants.

Originally, the organisation of prudential schemes to provide health and old age insurance for industrial workers was slow relative to Britain, Germany or the USA. For a long time, this delay was attributable to industrial workers' relative isolation within French society and the weak bargaining power of a constituency split between rival unions and political parties. Significantly the health and pension reform introduced in 1912 (but not implemented until 1928 and 1930)[19] only covered industrial and agricultural wage-earners (at a time when independent employment was still prevalent in these sectors). Moreover, as life expectancy was still relatively low (in the early 60s for males), the payment of social contribution was akin to gambling. Piecemeal assistance schemes introduced earlier by the Third Republic were generally limited in coverage and economical in provision; they included free medical assistance (the 'poor man's doctor'), the creation of orphanages (1904), and asylums for the destitute (1905), and the introduction of child benefit (from the fourth child) in 1932.[20] On the eve of the Second World War France was decisively left behind in terms of welfare provision (except in Alsace-Lorraine)[21] and military pensions dwarfed all other welfare benefits: nationwide unemployment insurance was not introduced until 1959.[22] Social contributions typically represented 8 per cent of the wage bill, and social transfers in total less than 2.5 per cent of GNP.

The 'social security ordinances' issued by the provisional government in 1944 proposed a complete overhaul of social insurance by decentralising its management among branch offices by area and profession. Hospitals were nationalised and put under a central government agency (*Assistance Publique*). Social security was thus construed as a separate administration, managed by elected boards (the first elections took place in 1947). Mutual or provident societies were brought in to assist in the provision of supplementary benefits. Under this scheme employers and employees contributed equally to health insurance and pensions; compensation for industrial injuries and child benefit were financed entirely by firms. Restricted at first to wage-earners, social insurance was progressively extended to independent farmers in 1961, the self-employed in trade and crafts in 1966 and to the unemployed in 1967. Entitlements were

[19] Lois sur les assurances sociales of 5 April 1928 and 30 April 1930.
[20] Conceived as a policy to reverse the declining birth rate, it was reinforced in the Code de la Famille (1939) which imposed severe penalties for abortion.
[21] As part of the German Reich the three *départements* recovered from Germany in 1918 enjoyed the comprehensive insurance scheme contained in the Bismarck reforms of 1881–4.
[22] Although some municipalities had introduced emergency unemployment relief in the 1930s.

subsequently increased in the 1970s (to cover parental leave, retirement at 60) and received a boost from Mitterrand's first administration which increased the minimum wage, pension and other benefits and allowances. In addition, a 'safety net' for the long-term unemployed (RMI) was created in 1988 along with rent relief (APL). There were close to two million RMI beneficiaries (receiving € 420 a month) in 1999. While health care costs and pension payments crept up relentlessly with an increasingly ageing population, all these programmes (including free medical care to the needy, the CMU and the APA) have added substantially to the fiscal burden. The share of social expenditure in GDP (30.8 per cent) is on a par with that of the Netherlands and one of the highest in the EU (second only to Scandinavian countries). As a result, social contributions by employers and employees have soared to represent, in 2000, 188 per cent of take-home pay compared to 127 per cent in Germany and 66 per cent in Britain. This, coupled with disincentives to joining the workforce (early retirement schemes and university grants), has raised doubts about the sustainability of the whole welfare system.

Chapter 5
The institutions of French capitalism

How societies organise economic activities is obviously crucial to their economic performance and the wellbeing of their members. As we have just seen, the French state took an early and intense interest in co-ordinating market activities. 'The idea that the state is responsible for the public good is indeed a typically French idea which baffles most Anglo-Saxons' (E. Suleiman). This attachment of the French to the vision of the state as the supreme arbiter of social processes and individual actions is put down to the country's historical legacy, its legal dispositions and, ultimately, its cultural preferences. But obviously, since France never attained the command economy stage, other institutions must be taken into consideration, those which operate the market or capitalist economy. A century ago Wilhelm Sombart (1863–1941) postulated a 'weak disposition of the French towards capitalism'. While this still constitutes a controversial proposition with regard to the nineteenth century, it seems that the postwar development of the French economy has proved the founder of the German historical school wrong. To be sure, a deep distaste lingers in the national consciousness for commercial transactions, and anti-capitalist pronouncements are commonplace (as the popularity of anti-globalisation campaigner José Bové has shown recently). The French, however, like most people, are eager to secure the benefits of competition as consumers while safeguarding their money as producers. For over a hundred years, successive republican regimes have tried to reconcile these conflicting aims by establishing a particular form of 'organised' or 'stakeholder' capitalism (in which the state supervises the allocation of income). However, the rhetorical insistence on curbing 'unbridled' market forces has not gone so far as to hamper the development of market mechanisms. Furthermore, the French brand of 'corporatism' is now unravelling in large segments of the economy, but is leaving in its trail a string of 'bad habits'. Neither Transparency International® nor the Heritage Foundation rank France very favourably in levels of corruption (21st) or economic freedom (39th). In addition, various institutional hurdles (including 'red tape') continue to hamper the foundation of new enterprises and to depress France's 'economic creativity index'. This has contributed powerfully to keeping the country down in 24th place among the advanced nations despite its commendable contribution to and/or rapid adoption of technological innovations. Perhaps France is another 'family with the wrong people in control' (George Orwell)!

1. Incorporation of new companies and entrepreneurship

As Polanyi's (1944) demonstration showed, the economic sphere of productive and commercial activities was gradually emancipated from political tutelage in the nineteenth century. This trend was reversed for most of the twentieth century until the late 1980s when a 'great re-transformation' was put in hand, mainly under the pressure of European integration and the internationalisation of financial flows (the so-called 1986 'big bang').

Until François Mitterrand's accession to the presidency in 1981, the avowed aim was for the state to terminate (Communist), reform (Socialist), or tame and organise (Neo-Gaullist) market forces, and consequently to monitor business creation and introduce guidelines for company management. Only recently has it become apparent that healthy entrepreneurship is directly connected with wealth creation. For a long time, firms and entrepreneurs were typically perceived as necessary evils which would provide gainful employment and tax revenues. Hence the strength and appeal, until the very end of the twentieth century, of corporatism,[1] the notion that all economic activities and professions (in theory – in practice only selected ones) could and should be protected from competition and organised so as to maximise their members' welfare.

---

[1] A notion in French historical literature still almost exclusively associated with the Vichy era. In its general acceptance it can in fact be viewed as a dominant feature of the organisation of production from Méline to Mitterrand.

Taking a different tack, most business historians have long advocated the notion that business creation is a major indicator of an economy's vitality, and entrepreneurs vital promoters of technological innovation and economic development. How has France fared in the long term in this respect?

French 'backwardness' before the Second World War was first ascribed to faulty entrepreneurship. A famous article by David Landes (1949)[2] sparked a debate which raged for a decade and still triggers occasional rebuttals by French business historians. His perception was that French family enterprise culture fostered conservative behaviour and risk aversion, and consequently thwarted innovation. This stance became (or was already) part and parcel of the 'Malthusian' behaviour of French business (or restrictionism) denounced by French interwar and postwar reformers. Jean Monnet, for instance, spurned the 'cult of the small-scale' and the provincialism of entrepreneurs.

Returning to this subject fourteen years later,[3] Landes noted that in his view, mentalities had changed tremendously in the course of a mere generation and emphasised the emergence and spread of 'new model' business attitudes and management in France. If there was any lack of capitalist vigour this does not seem to have been because French society (in its intellectual or mental dispositions) was incapable of fostering and nurturing able business leaders in sufficient numbers.

Neither does it seem to be attributable to the inadequacy of the legislative framework or case law as it developed in the twentieth century. Free enterprise always figured prominently in statute law and was indeed inscribed in the preambles of successive constitutions among the inalienable rights of man. The Code de Commerce, published in 1807, served as the basis of corporate regulation throughout the twentieth century and its laissez-faire inspiration is blatant. Business creation was mainly affected by constraints on the operating framework of existing firms (credit regulation, taxation, working conditions and so on). Generally, right-wing majorities in

---

[2] David S. Landes (1949), 'French entrepreneurship and industrial growth in the nineteenth century', *Journal of Economic History* 9/1, 45–61. Expanded on in Landes (1951).

[3] David S. Landes (1963), 'New model entrepreneurship in France and problems of historical explanation', *Explorations in Economic History* 1, 56–75.

Parliament have been sympathetic to business concerns, but were inclined to introduce business-friendly reforms only in times of economic prosperity. Three such periods spring to mind: the boom of the late 1920s, the mid-1960s and the late 1980s. Conversely, left-wing majorities have tended to do the opposite and have sometimes been inclined to go as far as outright spoliation (in 1924, 1936, 1945, 1981–2).

After nineteenth-century legislation gradually lifted restrictions on business incorporation while imposing strict legal and financial liability on management, the twentieth-century trend has been towards imposing conditions on incorporation while relaxing liability (mainly financial). Thus several amendments (in 1902, 1913 and 1930) to the law of 24 July 1867 liberalising stock companies were introduced to increase the flexibility and adaptability of corporations.

Most of these measures were aimed at strengthening existing companies rather than promoting the creation of new ones. During the First World War, as a concession to co-operative labour unions, Clemenceau's war cabinet legalised the distribution of shares to shopfloor workers, a foretaste of de Gaulle's 1969 failed reform on 'participation'.[4] Interwar case law by the *tribunaux de commerce** was decidedly tolerant towards business practices (insider dealing was common and tolerated). Many corporate scandals (among others the Marthe Hanau trial in 1928 and the Sacazan and Stavisky affairs in 1934) highlighted the naivety, sometimes bordering on connivance, of the judges.

New advances were made in the legalising of premium shares, warrant issues, share warrants, convertible bonds, index-linked (variable revenue) bonds and participating bonds, as well as the establishment of holding companies. A major legislative breakthrough occurred with the introduction of limited liability on the Anglo-Saxon pattern (the SARL) by the law of 17 March 1925 which greatly facilitated bankruptcy proceedings and, in the words of G. Ripert,[5] made 'the luxury of anonymity and fraudulent behaviour accessible to petty shopkeepers'.

---

[4] Defeated in the June 1969 referendum which sparked General de Gaulle's final resignation.

[5] France's major expert on corporate law (charged with treason, he was jailed at the Liberation).

Table 5.1 Distribution of French firms by corporate status, 1969

	% of total*	% of turnover
Limited liability	30.2	15.4
Joint-stock	21.6	68.3
Partnerships	3.1	2.8
Co-operatives	0.5	0.9
GIEs	0.05	0.03
Other	3.5	1.2
Individual businesses	41.05	11.37

* Total: 1,764,000 firms.

The introduction of limited liability and the liberalisation of joint-stock companies account for their rapid development from the late 1920s onwards; they substituted traditional forms of corporate organisation (especially partnerships) and became the dominant form of business structure during the 'Golden Age' after 1950. They went from representing 27 per cent of incorporated companies in 1920 to 34 per cent in 1936 to 52 per cent in 1969.

Business startups, depressed during the 1930s and the Second World War,[6] picked up during the reconstruction and expansion periods. Restrictions were eased; the legal status of limited-liability and joint-stock companies was unified, and standard bankruptcy and composition proceedings were adopted (laws of July–November 1966). From the 1973 oil crisis to 1985 the depressed economic environment and the government's economic strategy (increase in corporate taxation) together decimated French firms.

French commercial law has traditionally turned a blind eye to trusts, cartels and ententes. Rampant in manufacturing industry before 1914, these were officially recognised by law in 1926 and 'consolidation' was officially encouraged. While they sought to bring market discipline into the French economy, de Gaulle's ministers and *technocrates** remained favourable to concentration. The law of July 1965 triggered a spate of mergers more or less ordained by political fiat in the hope of creating 'national champions', but which

---

[6] The law of 16 November 1940 passed by the Laval government made the publication of board minutes and auditing by a certified accountant mandatory.

often amounted to extending a blank cheque to unprofitable 'lame ducks'.[7] With respect to concentration, it succeeded: of the hundred largest companies in the world, only one was French in 1958 (and ranked 98th); there were nine in 1970 (and still seven in 2000). This entailed cross-holding of equity and interlocking directorates. This trend was reversed after the first privatisation programme in 1986. Anti-trust law was belatedly and reluctantly taken on board after France was compelled to conform to the European Commission's recommendations included in the Single European Act of 1986.

2. The financial system

The French have long been regarded as inveterate cash hoarders since the trauma of runaway inflation during the French Revolution. This tendency, particularly conspicuous in the age of monetary stability (until 1914), survived for a generation and sustained a saving rate which showed no sign of abating for most of the century (it peaked at 20.2 per cent at the end of the Golden Age). Only recently has it lowered towards the Anglo-Saxon 'spend today, save tomorrow' pattern (12.6 per cent in 1998). In the interwar period bank accounts became more common among ordinary people, but the geographical dispersion of the population hampered their spread despite official encouragement. Meanwhile, post office savings banks opened throughout the country and payment by cheque was made compulsory (laws of 1918, 1924 and 1941) in certain cases. The comparatively slow diffusion of banking services in the first half of the century is assigned to interwar monetary erosion, government bonds crowding out the stock market, and the failure of 'mixed banking' (all the more surprising, according to A. Gerschenkron, in that this was originally a French invention).

Government control over banking and finance, already extensive by European standards before 1939, tightened thereafter. The Vichy banking law of 1941 sought to remedy the 'anarchy' of financial institutions in the turmoil of the 1930s and impose strict

---

[7] In steel-making, Wendel took over Sidelor, in banking the BNCI absorbed the CNEP, in aircraft SNIAS merged with SNPE between 1966 and 1970.

checks on bank creation and management. Postwar governments expressed the same concerns. The country's four major deposit banks were nationalised in 1945 in addition to the Banque de France,* which was put at the helm of the domestic banking 'system': it supervised the conversion of deposits into loans, set interest rates through its discount rate, set limits on bank reserves in cash and treasury bills, and fostered bank concentrations and mergers (there were 200 banks in 1946, but only 69 in 1972). At the same time, loans were granted to households for mortgages and to priority business ventures. During this period, roughly half of all borrowing was subsidised in one form or another while public and semi-public establishments together supplied 50 per cent of all productive investment. The rate subsequently fell to 16 per cent in 1968 but rose again to 40 per cent in 1980, a level which increased again thanks to injections of equity during the Socialists' first term (1982–5). Until the 1980s, exchange controls and inconvertibility of the franc for residents sealed off the domestic banking 'circuit'. The logic of government control was pushed to extremes by a short-lived nationalisation of the remaining private banks (1982–6).

The banking reform of 1966–7 had done away with the separation between deposit and merchant banking and loosened the bonds between the Treasury and the banks in the hope of boosting saving and investment as well as banking services (along the guidelines of the Armand–Rueff report of 1959). It also set up a stock-exchange regulator, the COB, in 1967. However, deregulation was slow to set in (although the number of bank accounts surged in this period); it was prompted by enduring negative interest rates (as a result of rising inflation) in the 1970s and 1980s which reverberated on bank profitability and forced the French market to open to international competition – from which French bankers expected to reap large benefits (see Table 5.2).

This was achieved by the law of 24 January 1984 which lifted the last restrictions and opened the door to universal banking: in its wake native and foreign merchant bank branches proliferated as high real interest rates spurred investors towards open market operations (the 1986 'big bang'). However, in spite of the liberalisation of financial services, by 2000, close to 40 per cent of credit allowances were still subject to government arbitration.

Table 5.2 Distribution of credit by main depositors, 1990 (%)

	France	Germany	Italy	UK
Commercial banks	36.3	27.8	49.4	26.5
Savings banks	14.9	39.2	15.6	56.6
Financial companies	27.7	3.6	35.0	–
Mutual funds[1]	21.1	19.4	–	16.9

[1] including building societies.

3. Training, education, and R&D

The diffusion, sophistication and variety of skills found in a nation's workforce determine to a large extent its 'comparative advantages'. In this view, France's postwar 'economic miracle' realised the hitherto only scantily tapped potential of the French population in terms of intellectual, technological and design skills and qualifications. Sources of 'human capital', however, are egregiously difficult to identify and quantify. Economic growth literature rightly emphasises the role of elementary education (the '3 Rs'), typically measured by basic literacy rates and years of schooling. But informal as well as formal training needs to be taken into account and here the measures are much less straightforward. In the twentieth century, as economies became increasingly sophisticated, the life cycle of technologies and know-how accelerated and educational systems had to adapt at increasing speed. Furthermore, there are other cultural factors which often tend to be taken for granted in the interplay of the process of education. The work ethic is to a large extent determined by patterns of ethical behaviour and moral values and by the personal satisfaction drawn from productive activity, but these are typically difficult to identify, isolate and qualify.

France possesses one of the world's most uniform and centralised educational systems. The bulk of education expenditure is allocated from the public purse to state (and private) schools under the supervision of the Ministry of National Education, a huge bureaucracy with over two million teachers and administrators.[8] Its pyramidal

[8] A 1970s quip was that this constituted the second largest army in the world after the Chinese, and in the 1990s a controversial education minister referred to it disparagingly as 'the mammoth'.

structure was determined by a pledge to offer 'free, secular, publicly funded and compulsory education' to all children (Ferry acts of 1881–2). At first private (mostly Catholic) schools were tolerated, especially in areas such as Brittany where they predominated. At the time of the Dreyfus affair (1894–1906) the Radicals under Emile Combes clamped down on schools run by religious orders and replaced them with state schools. Some independent schools managed to survive in small numbers and after the Second World War were increasingly drawn into the ambit of publicly funded education. State subsidies were first introduced by laws passed in 1951 (loi Baranger) and 1959 (loi Fontanet). After the Socialists' failed attempt at wholesale nationalisation in 1984, the government by a law of 1993 took on the salaries of private school teachers and made private schools eligible for (building) maintenance grants by local authorities.

The educational policy of the early Third Republic had aimed at achieving universal literacy and providing a uniform basic curriculum to all six- to twelve-year-olds so as to turn them into enlightened, responsible, loyal citizens. The objective was essentially political. Once this was achieved, the mandatory school leaving age was gradually raised from twelve (in 1924) to fourteen (in 1936) to sixteen (since 1959). By the 1980s, as Figure 5.1 illustrates, the vast majority of teenagers were staying at school until their eighteenth birthday. In the 1980s the government embarked on a policy of dramatically increasing higher education (the rise of unemployment in the 1980s encouraged this trend), and today France has one of the world's highest ratios of student numbers to total population: 80 per cent of eighteen-year-olds today obtain the *baccalauréat* (French equivalent of A-levels) and 40 per cent go on to university.

Primary education, dispensed in elementary schools set up in the later nineteenth century, performed well from the interwar period to the 'Golden Age'. Teachers trained at special training colleges (*écoles normales*) succeeded in bringing a progressively larger proportion of twelve-year-olds through the *certificat d'études* (a rough equivalent to the British Key Stage 2). Attainment levels have been dropping in recent decades, however, and, on one count, 30 per cent of students entering secondary education fail to pass elementary literacy tests. While the 3 Rs have long been insufficient for securing employment,

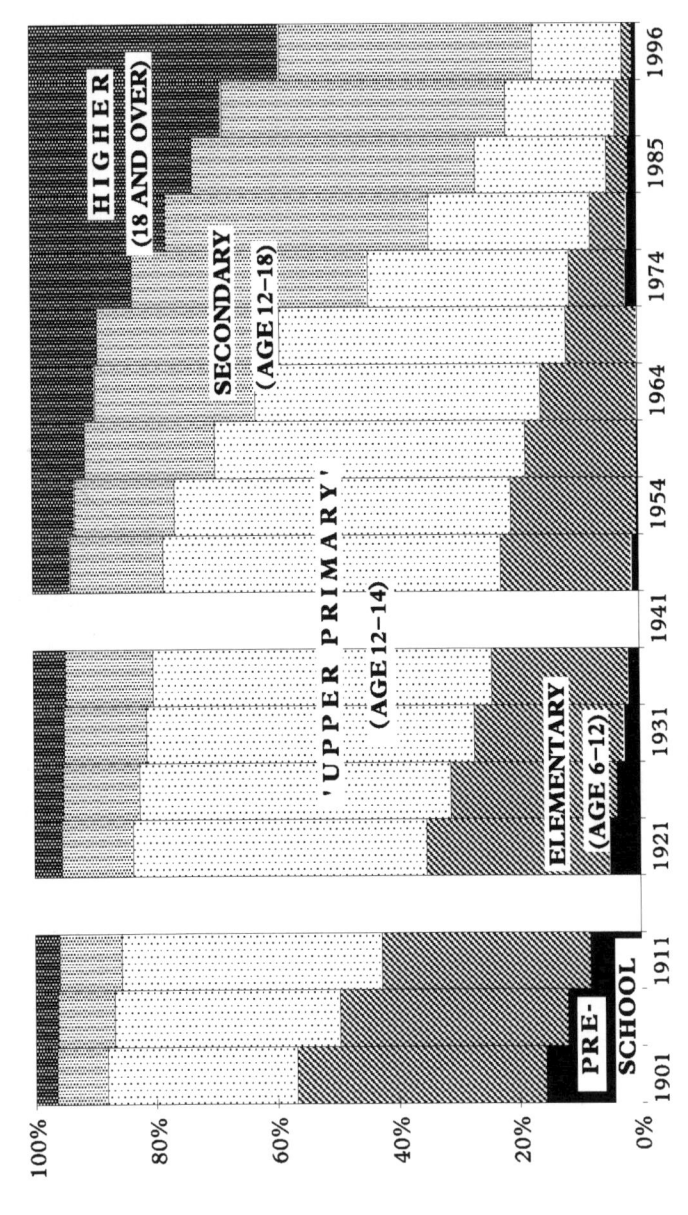

Figure 5.1 Education attainment levels by age cohorts 1901–96

The institutions of French capitalism 73

they are still essential for pursuing further education and vocational training. The bulk of government effort under the Fourth and Fifth Republics has focused on secondary education, acknowledged by education economists as being the most significant factor in human capital formation in an industrial society. Before the last war less than 20 per cent of teenagers attended secondary schools, split from 1941 between *collèges* (junior high schools) and *lycées* (senior high schools). France had fewer of them than Britain at that time, and about half as many students. The curriculum was heavily skewed towards the humanities and the 1959 Berthoin reform introduced *filières* (allocation) to classical, modern and technical schools on similar principles to the '11+' in the British Education Act of 1944. In 1975, in a bid to generalise secondary education, the Haby reform lifted the last hurdle between elementary and secondary education and introduced the *collège unique* (comprehensive school).

In the aftermath of the May 1968 student riots, the government vastly expanded the system of higher education (law of 12 November 1968, also known as the loi Edgar Faure). Previously, the French university system, designed at the end of the nineteenth century, had been based on a dual system of 'faculties' disseminated across the country and the elite *grandes écoles** network. Until the late 1960s there were fewer than a half million full-time students, half of them studying in Paris. Thirty years later their numbers had been multiplied by a factor of five across 77 universities.[9] Alongside them, a tiny minority of students had always been selected by competitive examination for admission into the *grandes écoles*, among which are the Polytechnique (est. 1794), Ponts-et-Chaussées (1747), Mines (1783), Centrale (1829), Normale Sup' (or ENS, 1794) and last but not least the ENA, founded in 1945 to serve as the springboard to executive careers in the civil service and on company boards. Partly owing to the lowering of standards in secondary schools, recruitment to the *grandes écoles* (unlike Oxbridge and the Ivy League) has not become more democratic; on the contrary, they are increasingly becoming the preserve of the offspring of alumni.

---

[9] Technical colleges (or *Instituts Universitaires de Technologie*), created in 1966, obtained university status in 1997.

Table 5.3 Domestic expenditure on R&D, its sources and performance indicators, mid-1990s

	Total ($bn)	Share of GDP (%)	Source (per cent) Government	Source (per cent) business	Research staff (thsds)	Patents[1] (thsds)
USA	268	2.70	29.8	66.8	965	2106
EU	162	1.81	36.8	54.8	858	na
Japan	103	3.10	19.7	72.6	625	435
Germany	51	2.38	35.6	63.5	238	544
France	**31**	**2.21**	**40.2**	**50.3**	**155**	**245**
UK	26	1.83	31.0	47.3	159	381

[1] registered abroad.

A century of government control and activism in education has crowded out private initiative, and alternative experiments have had to fit either inside the system or at its periphery. This is strikingly true of business and commercial schools. Since the end of the nineteenth century vocational schools have been created and maintained by professional and trade associations (e.g. Chambers of Commerce). They fostered the creation of business schools such as the HEC, ESSEC and others (fifty of them rank officially as *grandes écoles*); top schools such as the INSEAD now play in the same league as Wharton, Sloane and Harvard. In the 1920s, with the spread of the typewriter, the Pigier school made a speciality of teaching shorthand and typing.

How has the system affected performance in innovation and R&D? Technological innovation can be measured by the resources allocated to R&D, indicators of which did not become widely available until the second half of the twentieth century (Table 5.3). Since 1960 expenditure on R&D has averaged 2 per cent of GNP, broadly in line with comparable countries. Another measure of capacity, the number of full-time researchers, is also comparable to that in the UK or Germany. But they have tended to work predominantly in government agencies (the CNRS, CEA, CERM and others) in procurement, and in large corporations: in the 1990s large companies with government contracts, such as Aérospatiale, Thomson CSF and Alcatel, each spent over 10 per cent of their turnover on R&D. Likewise, the CNRS, originally created in 1939 but remodelled after 1945 after the Soviet Academy of Sciences, has gradually swelled into a huge bureaucracy whose members strive (not always successfully) for international distinction. By the end of the twentieth century, promising young researchers and professionals without the stamina or patience for job-rigging were increasingly trying their luck abroad, especially in America and the UK (witness the Nobel-prize-winning economist G. Debreu). France is thus subsidising human capital formation in other rival economies.

Most indicators are of capacity, and the impact of R&D on production systems is more difficult to assess. Ingenuity, however, can be appraised from circumstantial evidence relating to the frequency of inventions and discoveries, the granting of patents, and official distinctions. In the scientific[10] Nobel prize league, French scientists, with 27 laureates, have fared markedly worse than their counterparts in America (235), Britain (75) and Germany (62), but better than all other countries taken individually. France actually lost its status as a major scientific centre in the nineteenth century but a number of notable twentieth century inventions have been the products of French minds (see Table 5.4). The flow of inventions patented by French promoters abroad (in the USA above all) has shown no sign of abating and, though smaller, can be favourably compared with the German and British contribution. But since the 1920s and even more since 1945, process and product innovation has essentially been made possible by technological transfers from the USA, either directly or via subsidiaries of American multinationals. In the late 1940s productivity missions set up under the Marshall Plan met with great success and since then a constant stream of corporate executives has been exposed to American influence.

On the whole French businesses have proved good learners and conscientious emulators. The relatively low number of translations of books in English in technical subjects is also proof that readers can access them directly in the original.[11] Despite its inherent flaws, the evidence does not suggest that France's occasional shortcomings in R&D have come from funding, lack of ingenuity or inventiveness, or else negative attitudes towards innovation. Rather, an inadequate rate of business startups may be the result of

[10] Chemistry, physics, medicine and economics.
[11] In 1990 17.6 per cent of all technical books published in France were translations compared with 25 per cent in Italy and 14 per cent in Germany.

Table 5.4 Some notable French inventions and discoveries, 1890–1984

1891	pneumatic tyre	Michelin Bros.
1896	radioactivity	Becquerel
1902	scooter	Gauthier
1903	autochrome	Lumière Bros.
1906–23	BCG	Calmette & Guérin
1907	telecopy (fax) machine	Belin
1910	gearbox	Forest
1910	neon lamp	Claude
1912	dish washer	Labrousse
1915	armoured tank	Estienne
1922	shorthand (note taking)	Pigier
1926	aerosol	J. Estignard
1927	crepe rubber sole	Delbon
1927	cartridge pen	Perraud
1931	vegetable processor	Martelet
1937	artificial (iron) lung	Henry
1952	neuroleptic drug	Laborit
1953	pressure cooker	Lescure Bros.
1974	smart card	Moréno
1984	sun contact lenses	Essilor

the collusion and activism of entrenched interests, which have produced both barriers to entry and disincentives to business startups, as well as to the application of innovations.[12] It is estimated that, besides the expatriate personnel of foreign subsidiaries of French multinationals abroad, 150,000 French people, mostly young professionals, have set up shop in the south-east of England and 90,000 in California.

4. Corporatism, interest groups and collective action

The enduring strength, among French exports, of products of industries directly or indirectly dependent on government subsidies or protection, from farm produce to aircrafts, pharmaceuticals, and – last but not least – military equipment, hints at the existence

---

[12] In 2001, the administrative cost of incorporating a limited liability company was € 7,500.

of powerful corporatist forces; it also explodes the myth that the republican state extends equal treatment to all citizens 'regardless of creed, race, status etc.' J. Dessirier (1935) was among the first to pinpoint the existence of a 'dual' economy in which the performance of industries depended on whether they were 'sheltered' or exposed to the full savagery of the 1930s depression. Studying the causes of 1970s stagflation, Mancur Olson (1982), a public choice theorist, came to assign poor economic performance to 'social rigidities' brought about by the interplay of interest groups. French historians, while recognising the existence of 'lobbies' (Garrigues, 2002), have tended to play down their influence (to some, the notion that the state could be to a large extent manipulated by these groups is almost anathema). The paradox stems from the fact that common interest groups or *corps intermédiaires** are not recognised as having a legitimate voice in shaping policy-making. Some have, however, managed to carve themselves an influential role.

4.1 Labour unions

Historians of labour have devoted a great deal of attention to collective (or industrial) action and *syndicats* (unions, which were long perceived as marching in the vanguard of progress). Paradoxically, union representation has traditionally been weak in France by European standards. The rate of unionisation peaked in the immediate postwar period (35 per cent of the workforce in 1949), up from 20–25 per cent during the interwar period. But by 1958 it had fallen below the 1:5 ratio and it collapsed further in the 1980s, to 10.9 per cent in 1993, the lowest rate in the OECD. This weakness originally reflected 'under-industrialisation', and the dissemination of industrial employment among small *ateliers** and *fabriques** (and the consequent pressure to consent and conform) as well as the predominance of individualist values. Up to the Second World War, union membership was concentrated in large industrial plants such as Renault and Citroën on the outskirts of Paris as well as in the mining districts of the north, Lorraine and Saint-Etienne, in metalworking and in railway transport. Bitter strikes and walk-outs under union leadership characterised the early 1920s and mid-1930s.

In spite of a most celebrated motion known as the 'Charter of Amiens', passed at the first trade union congress in 1906, which

Table 5.5 'Representative' labour union federations and their representativeness

	Creation Date	Members (thsds)	Share of vote 1988 ballot	1997 ballot
CGT	1895	653	24.3	33.1
CFTC	1919	250	4.9	7.5
CGC	1944	196	5.8	5.9
FO	1947	1045	12.1	20.5
CFDT	1964	757	21.7	25.4

pledged to keep political and labour organisations separate, labour organisations have tended to align themselves with political parties, and political factors have played a major role in the development of the labour movement. The historic CGT split in 1920 between those who adhered to the guidelines of Lenin's Third International (and founded the CGTU) and those who remained faithful to the Charter of Amiens. In 1947, the foundation of Force Ouvrière (FO) was the outcome of the split between Communists and Socialists at the dawn of the Cold War.[13] Furthermore, under the 'social pact' established at the Liberation,[14] 'representative' (i.e. officially recognised) labour union federations were involved in decision-making, on the management of social insurance and labour–management disputes (a procedure known as *paritarisme**). The four (five from 1964) 'representative' federations played an important role during the 'Golden Age', in particular during the negotiations leading to the Accords de Grenelle* (1968). However, despite their stranglehold on representative bodies, their influence in the workplace has been dwindling ever since. Part of this decline is structural: unions typically represented unskilled manual workers in industries which have now declined; the surge in service jobs excludes union representation tacitly or practically (as recent strikes in the Accor hotel chain and fastfood outlets have illustrated). As a result, public service workers have increasingly provided the

---

[13] And of the consequent dismissal of Communist cabinet ministers (5 May 1947).
[14] 'The Liberation' refers to the period between the Normandy landings (6 June 1944) and De Gaulle's resignation from the government (23 January 1946).

backbone of union organisations and recurrent demonstrations aimed at defending their entitlements (including early retirement, generous pension benefits and security of tenure) now look increasingly perfunctory. Employers' associations have been even weaker and more fractious.[15] It was a government initiative by Etienne Clémentel (see portrait gallery) which brought about the creation, in 1919, of the CGPF, the employers' federation to provide business with a voice in the consultations between management and labour in the turbulent wake of the Great War. Bitterly divided by the Accords Matignon* (1936), it was refounded in 1946 under the new acronym CNPF, while a dissident organisation representing small and medium-size firms was set up separately (CGPME). Originally the mouthpiece for large and prestigious companies, the CNPF has gradually moved to represent the rank and file of French business in the 1970s and 1980s. Unlike in the German co-operative institutional arrangements, unions now appear increasingly marginalised, as just another galaxy of self-interested pressure groups.

4.2 Closed shops and anti-competition clauses

This category includes a number of 'special status' professions which enjoy some form of privilege or legal monopoly. In fact, the widening rift between 'sheltered' activities and those in the private sector, fully exposed to market forces, could be attributed to the continuing fractiousness and contentiousness of French society (Tilly, 1986). The largest component of this constituency is made up of the public services, including schools, hospitals, the post office, France Telecom,[16] Air France, the rail operators SNCF and RATP, the electricity and gas utilities and a cluster of organisations established before or after 1945: the national lottery (1933), the AFP press agency (1944), the press distribution network NMPP (1947), the weatherforecasters Météo France and the job placement agency ANPE.[17] Their advantages (security of tenure,

---

[15] Generations of historians took it for granted that this was not the case, since the capitalist state was obviously on the side of the capitalists!
[16] These enterprises have undergone partial privatisation – the state retaining a 'golden share'.
[17] In 1962 the government held monopoly stakes in forty different concerns in eleven different industries (from tobacco manufacture to potash and gunpowder).

promotion by seniority, union rights, government-funded pensions) were embedded in the statute of the public services in 1946. In addition, a number of professions enjoy some form of legal monopoly. In 1959 the Armand-Rueff report identified twenty-six 'closed shops' with substantial barriers to entry. Prominent among them are law officials such as *avoués* (solicitors), public notaries,[18] stockbrokers (their privilege goes back to 1681), bailiffs,[19] and auctioneers (limited to 328). The opening of pharmacies has also been subject to strict controls and official permission. Likewise taxis have been regulated since a law was passed on 13 May 1937 to remedy 'the anarchy of competition' (it limits the number of licences). Utility companies which were concessionary until 1945 – official car-dealers, petrol stations and supermarkets – have also been extensively regulated.

4.3 Technocracy

The Third Republic was nicknamed 'the republic of the professors'[20]; the Fourth was 'the republic of the comrades'; the Fifth Republic is increasingly becoming known as that of the 'technocrats', i.e. those whose superiority comes from their expertise. This term embraces different circles of people who wield a certain amount of power – economic, financial or political. Seen from the outside the closest historical parallel is the Soviet *nomenklatura*. Although commonly associated with the *énarchie* (a power structure made up of ENA alumni[21]), its core includes 238 *grandes écoles* (sixty-four of which are private establishments) which together churn out about 25,000 graduates annually. Technocrats are credited with having presided over, indeed engineered, France's postwar economic renaissance, gradually acquiring a hold over the *grands corps* in government, GENs and top executive positions in private corporations,[22] as well as sinecures in academia and the media. The phrase *étato-capitalisme* was coined recently to describe the cosy

---

[18] Solicitors entitled to deal with inheritances.
[19] Empowered to perform seizures or attachment of real property.
[20] Although barristers were over-represented in elected assemblies.
[21] Roughly equivalent to the 'Oxbridge connection'.
[22] By a procedure known as *pantouflage** (from the word for 'slippers') high civil servants could retire into company directorships.

arrangements between friends within the power networks.[23] The sociologist Michel Crozier observed (1960) that such relationships necessarily entailed significant losses in terms of efficiency, and Pierre Bourdieu (1977) emphasised the tendency of such organisations to engage in 'social reproduction': 'heirs' and insiders have the means and the incentives to secure control and bar undesirable outsiders from entry. The damage was limited as long as access to executive positions remained open to people of talent, but as upward mobility has stalled, these groups have been able to entrench their privileges and pass them on to their offspring or chosen successors, suggesting the pattern of a 'stationary society'. As in other countries the development of 'crony capitalism' has spawned recurring financial scandals, especially during the Mitterrand presidency. Pareto's second (and lesser known) theorem, according to which oligarchies have a natural tendency to bring about their own downfall, seems to have allowed for a number of exceptions so far, notably in the French case.

[23] Léon Say (son of leading laissez-faire economist Jean-Baptiste Say) predicted the emergence of such a power structure in his 1884 book *Le Socialisme d'Etat*.

Chapter 6
Labour: the French at work

Friedrich Sieburg, a keen observer of French culture writing in the late 1920s, expressed his admiration for the apparent detachment of the French from gainful pursuits (see p. 6). As in many other instances, the occasional visitor's testimony tends to distort reality. However, the endurance of an extensive traditional sector for over half of the twentieth century must be connected with the implicit and widespread preference for a rural lifestyle and the values associated with it; a backward-bending labour supply curve long reflected this preference for independence and leisure. But the transformation of French society after 1945 and its convergence on the Western European pattern carried with it changing attitudes towards work, employment and business. In the course of the twentieth century, the labour market underwent four major changes which were without precedent but which the French share with other OECD members: a sweeping change in the sectoral composition of the labour force, the rise of the proportion of wage-earners and women in the workforce, the continuous shrinking of working time, and, from the 1970s onwards, the rise of massive structural unemployment.

1. **From peasant society to postindustrial society in two generations**

The structure and outlook of the French working population was very different at the end of the twentieth century from what it had been in the first half of that century. Within a generation, the postwar 'Golden Age' transformed types of jobs, as well as working habits and living conditions, beyond recognition. Until the Second World War the majority of French people worked either at home or from home, in a familiar setting (among a small circle of relatives and friends) in rural or suburban communities; twenty-five years later France's traditional farming economy was vanishing fast and work now meant living in an urban environment and working in a distant factory or office.

1.1 Total employment

Compared to neighbouring countries, France's total working population remained relatively stable well into the twentieth century, hovering around a total of twenty million until the 1970s. In fact, total employment was lower in the mid-1950s than it had been in the mid-1920s. Until the postwar baby boomers reached adulthood in the late 1960s, employment in aggregate numbers was weighed down by the demographic stagnation of the first part of the century (or even going back to the 1880s).

From then on, numbers in employment gradually rose to twenty-three million in the 1980s before reaching twenty-five million at the end of the century; by 2010 it will have stoped increasing and reached a plateau. The working population would have expanded more dramatically had it not been for the measures taken to reduce unemployment: people of working age with admittedly few job prospects were enticed or moved out of the workforce.[1] As a result, France figures today among the countries with one of the lowest participation rates (measuring the proportion of adults of working age – eighteen to sixty-four years – actually employed).

By contrast, between the end of the First World War and the 1970s, the French economy needed to attract foreign workers to eke out its workforce. Belgian, Italian and Polish workers came during the interwar years along with Spanish republican refugees and Italian and Portuguese emigrants. This trend was reinforced in the 1950s–1960s by North African immigration (especially from independent Algeria and Morocco). With gaps in living standards widening between the rich nations and the underdeveloped world, the flow of immigrants has since greatly diversified, with French-speaking equatorial Africa supplying large numbers of (not

---

[1] This procedure replaced official redundancy (AAL), in force between 1975 and 1986.

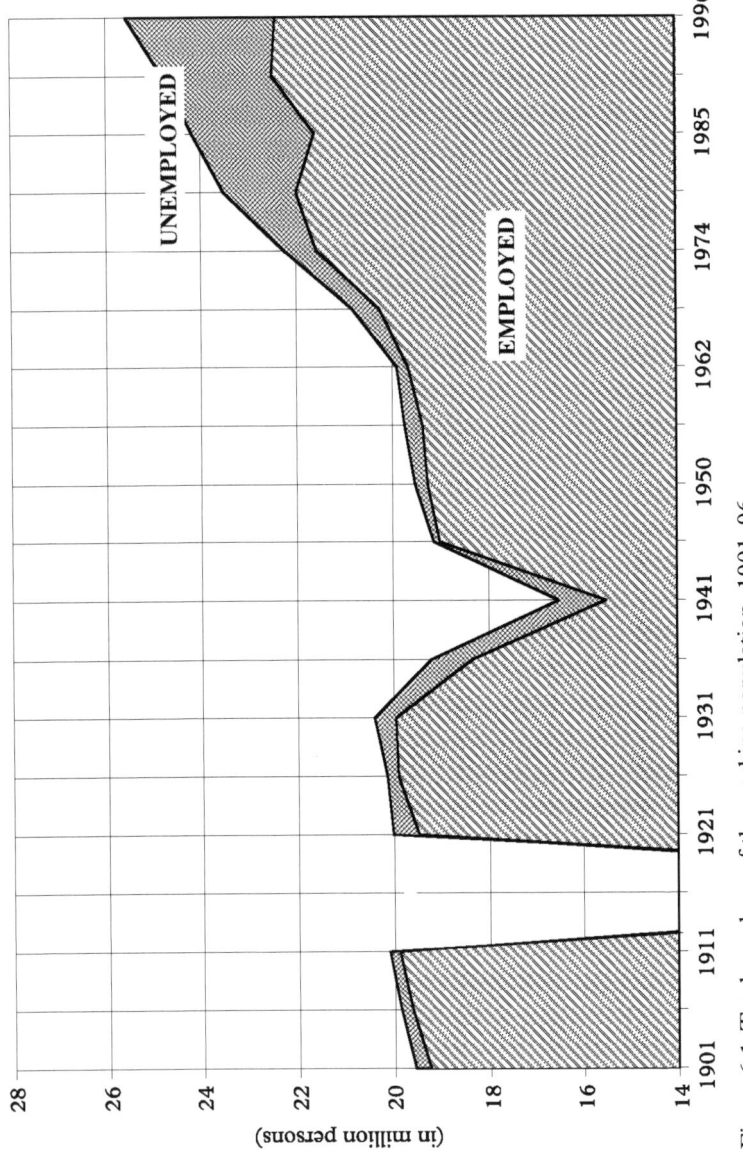

Figure 6.1 Total numbers of the working population, 1901–96

always legal) immigrants. Although France is now twice as heavily populated as it was in the middle of the nineteenth century, when much of its population lived in the countryside, economic activity is now disproportionately concentrated in the cities, which though they represent only 20 per cent of French territory are home to 80 per cent of the people.

1.2 The decline and fall of traditional activities

Jacques Tati's films (in particular *Jour de fête* and *Mon oncle*) illustrate, with a touch of melancholy, the final collapse of the traditional way of life during the postwar boom. *Jour de fête* (1946), filmed in a village in rural Touraine with a non-professional cast, screens a lifestyle which had only slightly altered since the turn of the century. Although rural migration to the burgeoning industrial and city centres had started as early as the 1840s, it involved relatively small numbers until the postwar 'Golden Age'. Irregular in timing, these migrations typically increased during economic booms in the urban industrial sector, only to slacken when economic conditions deteriorated (Goreux, 1977). Averaging 80,000 per annum between 1921 and 1936, final departures from rural areas significantly slowed down after the onset of the worldwide depression in 1930. In 1931, for the first time, half of the population was registered as 'urban', although towns with 2,000 inhabitants (a much lower threshold than in comparable countries) qualified as 'urban'.

At the time of the opening of the first Air France connection between Paris and New York (1949) a small majority of French people were still dependent on the traditional subsistence economy, which had hitherto proved spectacularly resistant to change. Postwar France, however, was poised to take a dive into fully fledged industrialisation and urbanisation.

1.3 Industrialisation in one generation

Between 1946 and 1973 rural migrations accelerated to a pace (135,000 annual departures on average) close to double that recorded during the interwar period. As this movement fuelled spectacular productivity gains in agriculture (6.6 per cent per annum until 1973), most of the migrants moved to burgeoning industrial

ÇA NE NOUS RAJEUNIT PAS...

– *My grandfather used to be a bonesetter*
– *And mine belonged to the Radical party.*
A cartoon by Monnier from *Le Canard Enchaîné*, 24 October 1945.

Figure 6.2 Wind of change after the 1945 election

centres – almost half of them to the greater Paris area. During the 'thirty glorious years' of the Golden Age, total employment in industry (including construction) increased by a quarter, to reach 8.3 million persons on the eve of the 1973 oil crisis. Part of this increase was mere 'catching up': in the mid-1960s the number of industrial jobs was pratically the same as during the late 1920s. Industrialisation accelerated thereafter, especially during the Pompidou presidency (1969–74), when a series of grand industrial projects were launched, among them the offshore steel-making complex at Fos near Marseilles. Tellingly, political decision-makers still conceived industrial development in pre-First-World-War terms: tons of coal, cement and steel still epitomised industry in their view. Accordingly, industrial output was heavily skewed towards the manufacture of semi-finished, intermediate and durable goods, mostly for the domestic market. Most of these industries used mature, stable technologies, but the scale of operation had radically altered since the interwar period. Concentration of production and economies of scale became a national obsession, and this is reflected retrospectively by the emphasis economic historians, from Caron to Sicsic, have put on the issue.

French industrialists sought constantly to increase their scale of operations, spurred on by public authorities which encouraged mergers and takeovers. Gradually, the system of customised flexible production was replaced by the assembly line and standardised mass production. France's 'traditional' industries such as textiles, iron and steel were thus reorganised and mechanised. In 1945 France's stock of industrial machinery was 75 per cent less than Britain's in size and was on average fifteen years older.

With hindsight, the most extraordinary feature of the 'French economic miracle' is that the industrialising effort was deployed in an ideological context that was both pro-growth and anti-capitalist. At the time, the vast majority of French people were convinced that their lot was deteriorating, not improving, contrary to what became evident after the event. Moreover, industry in this period provided a model of salaried employment which spread to other activities outside it, in addition to the '*métro–boulot–dodo*' (tube, work, bed) pattern derided by the cobble-throwing students of May 1968.

1.4 The rise and rise of postindustrial society

Just as the workbench epitomised the typical early twentieth-century working environment, the desk (soon adorned with the ubiquitous personal computer) epitomised that of the late twentieth century. In this respect, France followed the pattern of most OECD countries, but by the late 1980s it was among the leading tertiary economies. The expansion of services was all the more striking in the light of the slow growth this sector had experienced before the Second World War (25 per cent of GNP in 1881, 31 per cent in 1931). Since the war tertiary activities have tended to accelerate: between 1962 and 1996 ten million jobs were created in this sector, and in the 1980s, its growth was greater than in the first fifty years of the century. Two factors are usually emphasised to account for this rise. Firstly, Engel's law implies that, as personal income rises, consumption tends to shift from material goods to 'immaterial' services, geared to improving people's quality of life. Secondly, as the production of material goods becomes more complex, it requires an increasing number of operations anterior (design, research) or posterior (marketing, distribution) to actual throughput of materials. Other mechanisms can also interfere. Historians are sometimes too quick to see the tertiary sector as a shelter for 'unproductive' (or 'not directly productive') employment. Moreover, disguised unemployment is assumed to be more prevalent in the largest sector. But conversely, the expansion of France's services can be attributed to the realisation of comparative advantage in a broad range of internationally traded service industries (transport, telecommunications, insurance, public utilities), reflecting the sophisticated skills provided by the development of further education. The evidence for this is mixed, however: the boost in services could also reflect a falling off of industrial production.

2. Women in the workplace

One of the most spectacular features of twentieth-century social development in Europe has been the spread of female employment and the promotion of women to positions, either executive or operative, hitherto held solely by men. In this as in other respects, France appears at the crossroads, borrowing characteristics from both northern and southern Europe. At the beginning of the century, France had seemed to spearhead women's economic emancipation. The female participation rate was relatively high compared to most other European countries; women represented 46.3 per cent of the working population in 1911, which implied that 35 per cent of them were in 'gainful employment' (or 60 per cent if we relate the percentage to the female population of working age, fifteen to sixty-four), compared to 80 per cent for men at the same date. But women were still considered as politically immature, and France was among the last Western countries to adopt female universal suffrage (1946). While other countries caught up in terms of female participation, in France it remained remarkably stable until 1968. Participation rates even declined slightly during reconstruction in the 1950s, the 'baby boom' obviously encouraging more women to stay at home to bring up their children. However, after 1968, which signalled a lasting downturn in terms of fertility, women positively rushed into the labour market: two million of them between 1968 and 1999 (an increase of 25 per cent in absolute numbers). The strongest growth was recorded in the twenty-five to thirty-nine age group, which represented only 40 per cent of total

Table 6.1 Distribution of female employment by broad categories, 1938 and 1985 (%)

1938		1985	
Farming	33.1	White collar workers	50.6
Industrial workers	28.6	Managers	24.1
Shop or business owner	12.2	Industrial workers	13.9
Domestic service	10.9	Other	11.4

female employment in 1954 but 70 per cent in 1996. Four out of five found employment in services. Unlike their predecessors, motherhood did not induce them to abandon their careers (despite the introduction of paid parental leave by the Jospin government in 1997), while the development of post secondary education delayed their entry into the workforce. Thus the spectrum of work and positions filled by women changed drastically over the course of the century (see Table 6.1).

Meanwhile, inequalities between the sexes in the workplace have persisted (a 25 per cent pay gap on average in 2000). Women were comparatively less affected than men by the contraction of the labour market in the 1980s (see Table 6.5 below) but young women (aged eighteen to twenty-five) appeared to be at a greater disadvantage than men in obtaining their first job: unemployment in this category soared to 25 per cent and beyond. Thus, while sex discrimination retreated from the shopfloor and the boardroom as women were promoted in greater numbers to executive positions (where they have displayed qualities once thought to be the preserve of male colleagues), the bulk of those that have joined the workforce in recent years have been channelled into low-paid unskilled jobs.

3. Working conditions and training

3.1 *Less time, more pay*

With regard to average working time, the French appear to be among the laziest among Western Europeans, although the hourly – rather than annual – labour productivity of those actually employed is among the highest in the world. Indeed, France is one of the countries in which working time has been most extensively cut. Between

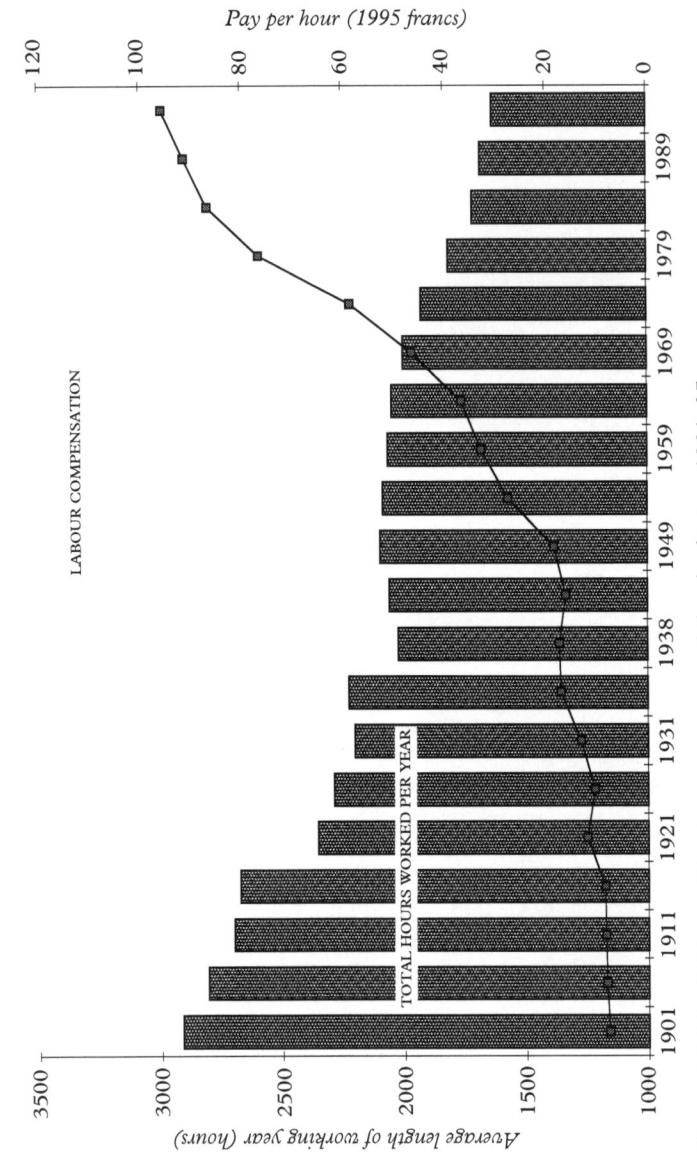

Figure 6.3 The fall in working hours per year and the rise in pay, 1901–95
* 'Pay' here means gross pay (take-home pay plus social contributions before tax).

1881 and 1989 the average working year was nearly halved (from 3006 to 1631 hours). This fall was continuous throughout the century, as is apparent from Figure 6.3. The service sector led the way (passing below the 2,000 hour threshold as early as 1938) while farmers lagged behind.

This reduction of working time is usually perceived as the beneficial effect of labour legislation passed in 1919 (bringing in the forty-eight-hour week), 1936 (forty-hour week) and 1982 (thirty-nine-hour week).[2] While a significant fall is easily identifiable in the 1920s, working time appears to have been held above the legal minimum during the early postwar decades. Surveys across professions through the 1950s indicate that the vast majority of French people accumulated overtime during the reconstruction and the ensuing 'Golden Age' (see Table 6.2, p. 92).[3]

In the meantime, workers' material conditions of employment and work greatly improved whilst payment in kind evaporated. Wage payments, direct and indirect, escalated in the postwar period, as the curve of Figure 6.3 illustrates: the average annual wage of a fully employed worker rose by a factor of 3.6 between 1946 and 1996 (on an hourly basis, by 5.9). By comparison, between 1896 and 1936 annual wage income increased by only 70 per cent (hourly wage rates doubled between 1913 and 1938). Nevertheless the Marxist dogma of the 'impoverishment of the proletariat' was still widely believed by trade unionists and intellectuals in the 1950s and 1960s.

The historical literature lays great emphasis on the *droits acquis** (entitlements) obtained by workers, usually after bitter industrial strife. In a context of labour scarcity and market rigidity prevailing over most of the century, workers and their representative organisations always found themselves in a strong bargaining position. This was the case during the First War, the 1920s (known as 'the golden age of the strike') and most of the post Second World War period. Unemployment (in the 1930s and 1980s) naturally dampened workers' demands and weakened their bargaining power. But union rights spread during the interwar period, with the most fearful

---

[2] A further reduction to thirty-five hours was passed in 1999 but has since been partially suspended.
[3] Between 1949 and 1953, fewer than 30 per cent of industrial employees worked less than forty hours a week and 10 per cent worked over forty-eight hours; 60 per cent worked between forty-two and forty-eight hours.

Table 6.2 Average number of annual working hours and weeks of paid holiday, 1913–90

Working hours	1913	1929	1950	1973	1990
Per week	51.5	49.0	45.3	44.7	39.0
Per year	2676	2287	2086	1923	1680
Paid holiday		1936	1956	1969	1982
Weeks		2	3	4	5

employers seeking to circumvent opposition by encouraging docile trade unions (known as *jaunes*). Between the Accords Matignon* (1936) and the Accords de Grenelle* (1968), which made union representation mandatory, advances in workers' welfare were mostly the outcome of tripartite agreements between employers, trade unionists and government representatives (under a procedure known as *paritarisme*[*4]). In 1945 the *comité d'entreprise** (works council) was made compulsory for all firms with at least fifty employees and was given advisory powers with regard to hiring and firing. Collective work contracts were generalised by a law of 1971 which further standardised hiring and firing procedures; this in turn encouraged a definite trend towards fixity of tenure, automatic pay rises and job security.

In 1950 a minimum wage (SMIG) was introduced; in 1959, a nation-wide scheme (UNEDIC-ASSEDIC) was set up to manage and distribute unemployment benefit. This was subsequently extended in 1978. In 1967, a network of ANPEs (job centres) was organised to provide placement information. Its performance has dwindled with the surge in unemployment and temporary work contracts; it compares unfavourably with Adecco, Manpower and Vedior-Bis, the leading placement agencies.

The energy crisis of the 1970s and the spread of de-industrialisation turned the tables and prompted a deterioration of both workers' earnings and their conditions of employment. Ironically, in 1973, the year of the first oil crisis, the government set up an Agency for the Improvement of Working Conditions (ANACT). Nevertheless, in the long run it was labour which bore the brunt

[4] see Chapter 5 (p. 78).

Table 6.3 Distribution of primary (PI) and disposable (DI) income between 1970 and 1997

	1970		1997	
	PI	DI	PI	DI
Households	74.6	70.9	74.5	69.8
Administrations	13.9	19.8	11.9	18.4
Companies	10.3	8.2	11.9	9.8

of the global shake-up in the production system. The share of the wage bill in value added peaked in 1982 (at 68.8 per cent) but subsequently spiralled steeply down to a trough in 1989 (59.3 per cent). Conversely, the distribution of total disposable income shifted in the direction of corporations, which in the 1980s and 1990s recouped some of their losses in terms of disposable income at the expense of households (Table 6.3). However, the margin between primary and disposable income remained practically constant which suggests that the lion's share of this increment was diverted into public transfers.

The deterioration was worse for those kept out of full-time employment. To stem the surge of unemployment among the young, the Socialist government introduced an array of temporary measures, such as TUCs (short-term labour contracts financed by local authorities) in 1985. In the following year, the then right-wing majority reversed this policy and passed a law on 'job flexibility' which successive governments, left and right, have found difficult to reverse in spite of electoral promises. The hardships encountered in and out of the workplace may explain why the French have become the world's largest consumers of tranquillisers. Stress, no longer limited to the workplace, now seems to have diffused through people's entire existence.

3.2 Training and skills

On the basis of the evidence collected by labour economists (Marchand & Thélot 1991), the quality of human capital[5] greatly

---

[5] Measured here by the numbers employed multiplied by the average length of schooling.

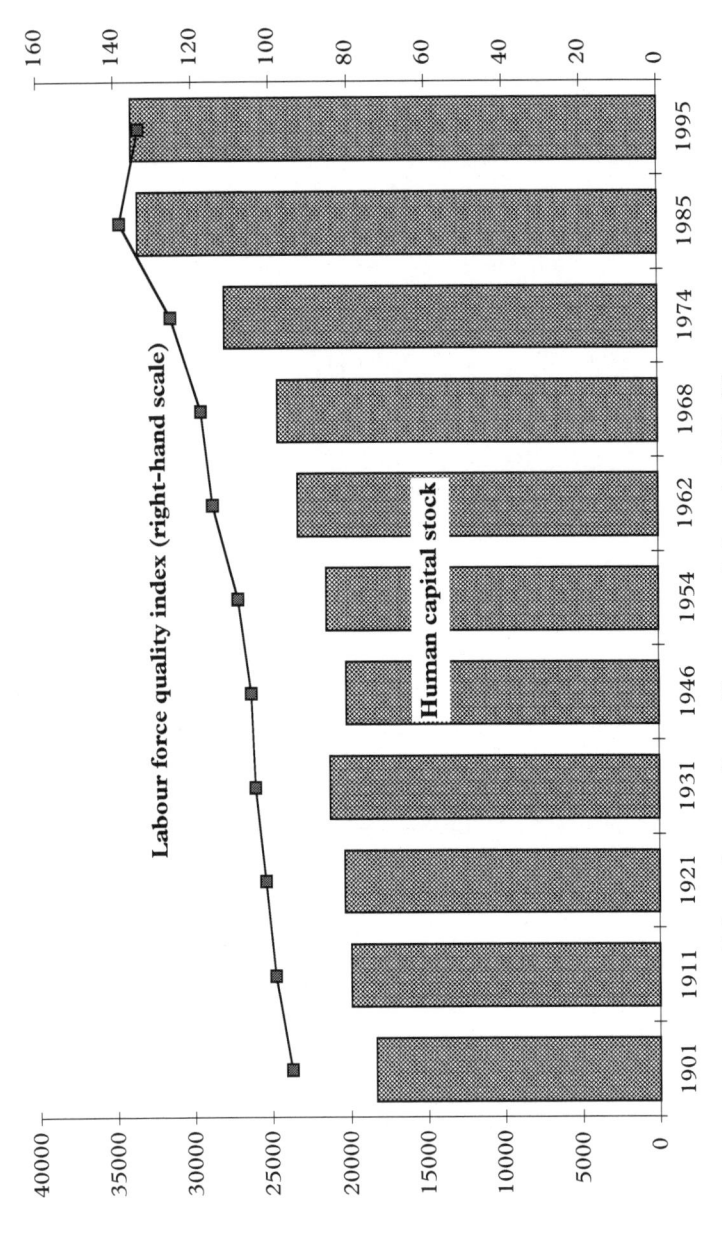

Figure 6.4 Measures of labour force quality and human capital stock, 1901–95

improved in the course of the twentieth century: by some measures, its stock has more than doubled since 1900 (implying an average increase of 1.1 per cent per annum over a hundred years). Qualitatively, however, the improvement is less dramatic (any given individual was deemed to be 35 per cent better off, in terms of skills and capabilities, in 1995 than in 1901), but comes across unquestionably – although progress seems to have levelled off in recent years (Figure 6.4).

This improvement took place disproportionately after the last war – an experience shared by most Western countries. At the end of the twentieth century schooling took up twice as many life years as it had a hundred years earlier, and between 1936 and 1996 the average number of years spent at school escalated from 7.5 to 12.4.

Measuring the link between increased investment and efficiency gains (which will normally push up earning capacity) is always somewhat tricky. For the 1970s, the evidence points to a marginal superiority of the French system over its American counterpart (Table 6.4). Indeed, until then the French *baccalauréat* (secondary school diploma) was widely accepted as equivalent to the Bachelor of Arts degrees dispensed by most American undergraduate colleges. This may have represented a swan song, however: the widening gap in productivity between France and the USA in the 1990s suggests a creeping improvement in the American educational system. This trend may be the reflection not so much of the efficiency of the education system *per se* as of the work ethic and working attitudes, which are not dispensed at school or in training classes but are diffused by the family and social environment. In France, the strong egalitarian and anti-capitalist bias of public education may handicap school-leavers as they enter the job market. There are hints, besides, that French education is now producing diminishing returns. Surveys of academic performance and placement tests suggest that the education system worked adequately up to and including the period of mass standardised production so long as demand was strong for low-skilled jobs. But its performance may have fallen below expectations since. Indeed, it is being increasingly challenged by the decisive shift away from commodity production towards the information economy and the resulting pressure to upgrade and diversify scientific, technical, and professional training. The persistence of high unemployment reflects, in part, the inadequacy of

Table 6.4 Productivity bonus by level of education, France–USA, 1977

	No schooling	4 years	5–8 years	9–12 yrs	13–16 yrs	17+ yrs
France	1	1.14	1.36	1.86	2.43	3.14
USA	1	1	1.21	1.41	1.75	2.42

training provision: to some extent the latter is preparing youngsters for the 'wrong' kind of jobs.

4. Unemployment

In the most advanced economies, unemployment emerged, and was identified as such, only during the 'Great Depression' in the latter part of the nineteenth century. In France, where industrialisation and full-time jobs were not yet as common as in Britain ('double occupation' and temporary or casual work were widespread), it took another generation or two for joblessness to be acknowledged as a social problem. Previously the unemployed had been assimilated with the floating population of homeless vagrants, travelling gypsies or entertainers, and were left 'unclassified'. From the 1906 population census, it can be estimated that the officially unemployed (mainly male workers in the industrial sector) numbered between 250,000 and 300,000, but Charles Gide (1847–1932), a contemporary economist, contended that the figure could safely be pushed to half a million workers. In the absence of either a national survey or any relief programmes (other than charitable or local initiatives), this could only be a rough, albeit informed guess. However, it suggests that unemployment in France long remained at the level of what is considered 'natural' or frictional unemployment.

In fact, for most of the twentieth century, the French job market suffered from a dearth of applicants, not of opportunities, as an effect of the population crunch between 1880 and 1940. Since the late nineteenth century France had 'imported' unskilled immigrants, most of them to work in its factories (see Chapter 1). This situation lasted until the baby boomers came of age and entered the labour market in droves in the early 1970s. Since then the problem has been just the opposite: the economy has proved unable to generate new job opportunities at the rate demanded by the population increase (see Figure 6.1).

In the traditional agrarian economy, pockets of underemployment were numerous: on farms and in workshops[6] relatives were sometimes employed at odd tasks, or else business was slack for recurrent periods during the working year. As industrialisation proceeded, unemployment became more conspicuous as well as more painful economically. It reached a first peak during the first postwar slump but relaxed in the late 1920s (the first unemployment support scheme was introduced by the Laval–Tardieu laws of 1928–30). The full impact of the 1930s depression on the job market was felt belatedly in the French case. While unemployment peaked in the US, Britain and Germany in 1932–3, in France its zenith was not reached until 1936 (850,000 out of work, or 7 per cent of the working population). Neither does this figure represent the full impact of the slump: an estimated 1.3 million jobs were destroyed in this period, but workers responded either by leaving the workforce (the participation rate fell to unprecedented lows), or by retreating to their home towns (native French people) and hence to the farm economy, or to their home countries (foreign workers).

After the war, confounding most predictions, which reckoned on a return to mass unemployment, the economy operated at full capacity in the 'Golden Age': in the 1950s and 1960s the joblessness rate sank again to its 'natural' level despite short (and minor) bouts of 'Keynesian' unemployment (due to weak demand), as in the summer of 1963. In the early 1960s, the labour market absorbed 400,000 refugees from Algeria without so much as a dip. As in Britain, however, job destruction began to creep upwards in the late 1960s, anticipating the blow inflicted by the first oil crisis of 1973; thereafter unemployment rose slowly but unremittingly from 1.6 per cent in 1966 to 3 per cent in 1973: there were already half a million unemployed on the eve of the OPEC price hike. Since the ensuing recession, from the second half of 1974, unemployment has risen continuously with only temporary remissions (between 1987 and 1990, in 1994–5 and between 1999 and 2001). What is worse,

---

[6] In this connection the standard measures of 'total hours worked annually' is somewhat misleading.

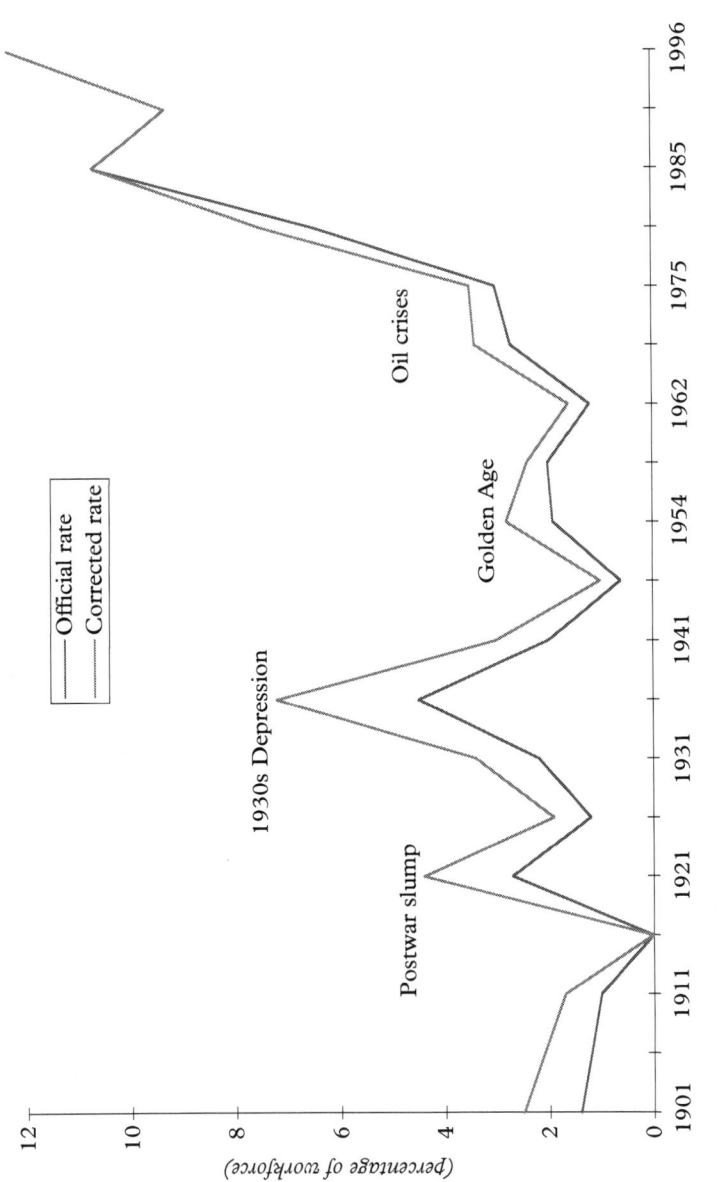

Figure 6.5 French unemployment rate across a century

Table 6.5 Unemployment rates by sex and age categories, 1986 (%)

	France	Italy	Germany	UK
Total unemployed	**10.1**	10.0	7.1	10.9
Men over 25	**6.0**	3.2	5.3	9.1
Men under 25	**20.4**	26.3	8.4	19.8
Women over 25	**9.8**	8.4	9.1	8.2
Women under 25	**25.7**	42.4	11.2	16.3

according to analysts, is that French unemployment has reached ever higher levels at each successive trough in the business cycle. De-industrialisation in the 1980s produced cohorts of long-term (over a year) unemployed, and early retirement schemes have been introduced to offset the inability of mature (fifty-plus) unskilled workers to re-enter the job market. At the other end of the spectrum, unemployment has disproportionately affected young entrants. In 1985 one in eight of the eighteen to twenty-five age group was out of work (23.2 per cent); hence the popularity of government-funded training schemes. With respect to employment, France now finds itself in the same situation as countries such as Italy and Spain.

While unemployment has been particularly prevalent among low-skilled (shopfloor) workers (13.7 per cent in 1985, 15.3 per cent in 1995), it has begun to affect *cadres** (managers) as well: unemployment in this category reached 4.6 per cent in 1999. By 2000, a higher education degree, long considered a bulwark against unemployment, no longer guaranteed a career and the unemployed graduate working in a 'junk job' has become a cliché in the press. But unemployment would have been far higher had it not been for the assistance provided to a growing section of the labour force under government schemes. In 1973, the beneficiaries of these measures geared to supporting employment numbered only 103,500; in 1999 there were two million. Between 1973 and 2000, government expenditure to prop up employment went from € 1.6 billion (or 0.9 per cent of GDP) to € 58 billion (or 4 per cent of GDP). In a typical boom year, such as 1999, with a buoyant labour market, the government still subsidised around 120,000 jobs. Thus, job creation remains weak and is skewed towards short-term positions: in the 1990s while the number of tenured jobs increased by a paltry 2 per cent, CDDs (eighteen-month contracts) and (subsidised) training courses rose by 60 per cent and 65 per cent respectively, and temporary employment surged by 130 per cent.

While timid on labour market reform, successive governments have taken comfort in the prospect that from 2010 onwards the working population will 'naturally' stabilise, hence normally allowing the reabsorption of high unemployment. But maintaining a large proportion of the workforce on the edge of the labour market entails costs in terms of lost output and income: with fuller employment the profile of the French economy would have been radically different from what it is today.

Chapter 7
Plough and pasture: lifeblood or drain?

For most of the twentieth century French school children were taught a quotation attributed to the Duke of Sully (1559–1641)[1] to the effect that 'plough and pasture are the lifeblood of France's economy'. This early 'physiocratic'[2] affirmation of the supremacy of agriculture over other economic activities curiously survived into the late twentieth century despite the ever-dwindling importance of farming in modern, industrialised economies. Although endowed with some of the best soils in Western Europe, France failed to achieve self-sufficiency in major foodstuffs until the 1960s (by which time the diversification of tastes was making this objective pointless). Fortunately (?) the CAP (Common Agricultural Policy), implemented in 1962, came to its rescue by granting French agriculture a second lease of life, and promoting France to the position of 'agricultural superpower' in Europe and the second largest exporter in the world. Recently, however, EU budget constraints and the industrial methods developed in animal farming (as well as the damage done to the environment) have cast doubts on the sustainability and ultimate soundness of a policy of massive public support to agriculture 'at any cost'.

1.   A 'ruralist utopia'[3]

Something curious happened between the middle of the nineteenth and the middle of the twentieth century: France, unlike many

---
[1] A companion and minister to King Henri IV (1589–1610).
[2] A school of pre-classical economics which argued that nature (*physis*) was the source of all material goods and consequently human-made wealth. Cf. Quesnay (1694–1774), *Tableau économique de la France* (1748).
[3] A phrase coined by the sociologist Henri Mendras in his seminal work *La fin des paysans* (1967).

101

comparable European countries, maintained, even after the initiation of industrialisation, a relatively high and stable labour force in agriculture. In 1936 there were about as many people employed in farming as there had been in 1866. Until 1946, a third of the country's workforce seemingly had jobs on traditional, mostly marginal, farms, depressing agriculture's global productivity. At the same time, food production was increasingly failing to meet demand from domestic (let alone foreign) consumers as their consumption patterns diversified. This did not detract the 'bread-eating public', all distant or recent descendants of farmers, from adhering – in the teeth of the evidence – to the belief that traditional farming was one of the country's strengths and was a *sine qua non* for the maintenance of France's *art de vivre*, especially its cuisine. Since the late nineteenth century, government support for agriculture, in the form of trade protectionism and price fixing, has reflected the popular consensus. While the emotional attachment to traditional forms of farming has its roots in the collective psyche and cultural representations, the persistent resistance of farmers to rural emigration can be attributed to the weakness of the demand from the modern urban sector or, alternatively, to the stubborn peasant's refusal to adjust to changing economic conditions or his pride in 'producing little and dear'. This behaviour can also be traced to the inhibiting effect of particular institutions, notably egalitarian inheritance laws. By clinging to traditional farming practices, farmers also expressed, in their attachment to an ancestral way of life, a preference for apparently 'irrational' choices in exchange for 'non-economic' advantages (such as choice of residence or economic independence). This preference, however, was paid for by generally harsh and sometimes 'primitive' living conditions; in this respect, women (farmers' wives especially), anxious to take advantage of the amenities of modern life, were to play a crucial role in the decision to migrate. Furthermore, the electoral system (district-based two-round majority ballot) ensured the over-representation of rural constituents so that no politician in his right mind could afford to ignore or confront the 'peasant vote'. To the public at large, agriculture corresponded to the ideal of self-reliance and 'balanced growth' – as politicians then formulated it: this fuelled the imagination of urban dwellers with dreams of the healthy, quiet bucolic life (hence 'rural utopia'). Torn between two contradictory goals – export on world markets at

Table 7.1 The effects of urban migration on labour productivity, 1896–1999 (annual change in %)

	Change in labour input		Labour productivity growth	
	gross	net	per annum	per hour
1896–1911	−0.4	−0.6	1.2	1.4
1921–31	−1.2	−1.7	2.4	2.9
1931–49	−0.6	−1.1	1.4	1.9
1949–61	−2.9	−3.2	6.5	6.8
1961–73	−4.4	−4.5	6.4	6.4
1973–79	−3.4	−2.8	4.0	3.5
1979–99	−3.1	−4.0	4.9	5.8

world prices or supply the domestic market at substantially higher home prices – French agriculture was prone to repetitive crises: one year harvest failures sucked in imports; bumper crops sent prices and incomes spiralling down the next.

Through the first half of the twentieth century, the structure of French farming continued to reflect the once-dominant traditional subsistence economy. On the eve of the First World War there were about five million (mostly family) holdings, 70 per cent of which were smaller than five hectares (12.3 acres). Only 1.5 per cent of all farms surpassed 50 hectares (125 acres). Of the 8.5 million people employed in this sector at the time there were 3.2 million farm labourers (of which close to a million were domestic servants and 750,000 journeymen); the rest were overwhelmingly small owner-occupiers. Subsistence farming was the rule but implied either low standards of living or additional income from casual sources. Yields were markedly inferior to those in neighbouring countries and so was the productivity of labour (half the British level).

Official government policy was geared to preserving a 'balanced' domestic economy to the avowed benefit of agriculture, but this locked it into a contradictory and insoluble predicament. On the one hand, it pursued the aim of self-reliance and self-sufficiency by restricting food imports (especially basic foodstuffs such as wheat, meat and wine); on the other, domestic farming proved incapable of satisfying the country's needs. Despite trade barriers, the trade deficit worsened every time harvests fell short of domestic demand, but surpluses brought about by bumper crops could not be exported at world prices. This policy also encouraged farmers to stick to traditional crops (in a move to minimise risks) at a time when urban customers' tastes were gradually shifting towards animal proteins, quality wines and fresh produce.

During the First World War agriculture was largely left in abeyance (three quarters of its workforce were in the trenches), and the gap in production was filled by massive imports under state control; this situation lasted until 1921. In 1918, as a result, agricultural output represented a mere fraction of its prewar level. It subsequently suffered a 'cost–price squeeze' as tariff protection was eroded by price inflation. It recovered in the latter part of the decade after the introduction of a new tariff in 1928. Farmers enjoyed a short spell of prosperity, taking advantage of the new franc parity which cut their debts in real terms.

In 1930, the depression in world trade hit agricultural produce first and hardest. Within four years, world prices for staples such as wheat and wine slumped by 50 per cent and 65 per cent respectively. Trade barriers, erected by the 1928 tariff, were raised again, but proved insufficient, and government had to intervene further in the face of growing discontent and activism on the part of farmers. In 1934, Roland Dorgelès organised, supposedly along Fascist lines, a *Front Paysan* (the 'green shirts') for the militant defence of farmers' interests. In order to reduce foreign imports, import quotas and export subsidies were introduced from 1931[4] along with non-tariff barriers (in the form of sanitary controls). To regulate the domestic supply, ever more complex price-support schemes were implemented whereby the government undertook to purchase unsold surpluses: wine was distilled to make methylated spirits and grain turned into ersatz petrol. This effort culminated in the creation of marketing boards for sugar, wheat and other cereals (ONIB, later ONIC) in 1936–7: even the Popular Front coalition of Socialists, Communists and Radicals could not afford to ignore the plight of a good third of the French populace. These measures paved the way to the fully fledged corporatism of the Vichy government, which established government control over the food supply and enrolled every

---

[4] The first 'import surtax' was issued following the devaluation of sterling in September 1931.

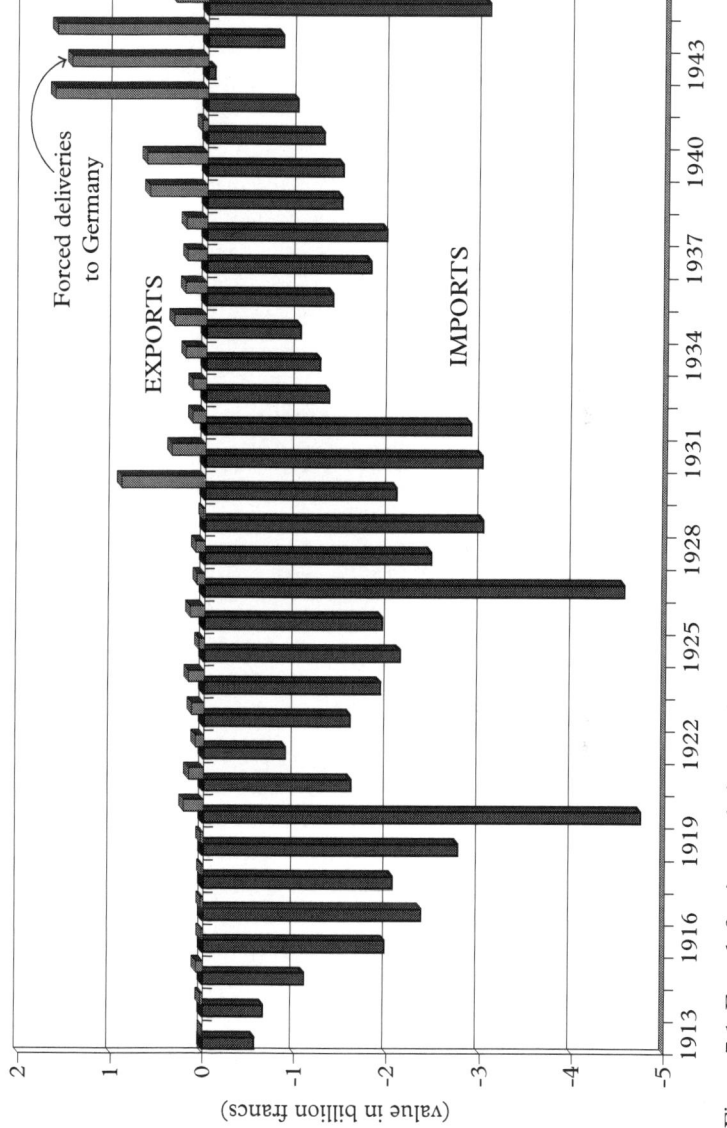

Figure 7.1 French foreign trade in cereals, 1913–45

farmer in the *Corporation Paysanne*. During the Second World War the sources of imports dried up and rationing was introduced, not least owing to compulsory deliveries to Nazi Germany. Shortages of basic foodstuffs were acute in most cities, especially in Paris and the south, despite the rapid development of the black market.

Until the last war the supposed 'lifeblood' of France's economy failed to ensure self-sufficiency in basic foodstuffs and/or to provide export earnings: the country's food supply even deteriorated markedly compared to the pre-First World War era, as if continued protection had actually encouraged further dependence on government. 'High farming' (intensive rather than extensive cultivation) failed to spread beyond a handful of farms and regions. Agricultural machinery and fertilisers[5] were a rarity and farmers' habitual bias was towards living frugally and hoarding cash (with a view to buying land in order to eventually consolidate their tenure); meanwhile the distribution of holdings had hardly changed since the end of the last century. In 1946 Jacques Tati's film *Jour de fête* showed Sainte-Sévère villagers still harvesting with scythe and sickle.

2. An agrarian revolution – of sorts

After the Second World War, making up for the wartime shortfalls in food production became an imperative: in 1947, the production of basic foodstuffs and the average individual calorie intake were lower than at any time during the war. German seizures, the collapse of the transport infrastructure and the fast-eroding value of the currency had encouraged farmers to sell their surpluses on the black market where prices were higher (between two and six times the current official prices); despite its doubtful effectiveness, wartime rationing had been extended to a large array of necessities. To reform this situation, postwar governments decided (as with industrial staples) to intervene in order to promote agricultural efficiency and hence improve the domestic supply of basic foodstuffs. The objective was to boost productivity and guarantee the profitability of crops so as to keep farmers in business over the medium term.

---

[5] The intake of phosphate and nitrogen-based fertilisers per hectare barely increased between 1913 and 1946; only potash came into wide use during the interwar period.

Table 7.2 Distribution of farms according to size, 1955–98 (in hectares[1])

	1955	1970	1988	1998
Over 50,000	95	131	172	192
10,000–50,000	913	755	455	244
Under 10,000	1299	702	390	244
Total	2307	1588	1017	680

[1] 1 hectare = 2.471 acres.

A series of reforms was introduced to foster the creation of larger farms (land consolidation), and access to credit (subsidised lending by the Crédit Agricole). A research institute, the INRA, was set up to experiment with and publicise new breeds, and a sizeable proportion of Marshall Plan aid was devoted to distributing fertilisers and all-purpose mechanical equipment. Between 1946 and 1966, the number of tractors in operation was multiplied by a factor of sixteen (from 60,000 to one million) and of combines by five (to 120,000). To enable smaller farmers to share in the investment, the government encouraged the setting up of co-operatives for the use of farming equipment (CUMAs). The government's target, however, remained the medium-sized family farms. Cultivators on smaller farms deemed unprofitable were expected to leave the land in the near future. While regionally based organisations (SAFERs) sought to set up young farmers on consolidated farms, ageing farmers were encouraged to retire on a lifelong allowance (IVD). Although the flow of land leavers increased in the 1950s, there remained until the 1980s an 'abnormal' proportion of very small farms: 'by the mid-1960s French agriculture was still encumbered with very poorly-equipped farms, low yields and a structural trade deficit, a situation not very different from its pre-WWI predicament' (Eck, 1994: 214).

At the end of the production line, the government introduced an ever more complex system of marketing boards with a view to ensuring the distribution of farming output at profitable and reasonably stable prices. While tariffs were pitched at unprecedented highs in the 1950s, the price-fixing mechanisms first tried out with wheat and other cereals in 1936 (the ONIB) were progressively extended to a great variety of crops and produce (milk, wine, sugar beet). This was first implemented in 1953 and was extended in 1960 with the creation of FORMA, a government agency in charge of purchasing and eliminating unsold surpluses. Although this policy was to benefit first and foremost larger production units in the agriculturally richer regions (Beauce, Brie, Picardy, Burgundy), it also provided a lifeline for a number of smaller, mostly marginal farms. On the eve of the creation of the CAP, the powerful farmers' union FNSEA (dominated by large landowners) managed to obtain a promise that it would be involved in all future decisions regarding agriculture (lois Pisani of 1961): in their view the way forward was clearly towards greater involvement of the public authorities (and purse) in the farm economy.

3. From deadweight to deadlock

Most historical accounts of postwar French agriculture depict it as a success story occasionally tinged with a touch of nostalgia for the 'world we have lost'. No general account has tackled the balance-sheet of agricultural modernisation with a cost–benefit analysis. At the time of the Pisani laws (1961–2), what was originally an economic problem gradually turned into a social and economic one. Productivity gains in farming were spectacular in the 1950s and 1960s (Table 7.1). All the same, the gap in income between agricultural and non-agricultural workers kept widening whilst production costs escalated, raising the cost, in real terms, of staple foods at a time when people's diet was diversifying. As a result, farm incomes were not catching up on non-farm, urban ones: despite occasional bursts of prosperity they were, on the contrary, left behind. This fuelled the militancy of farmers' unions, which pressured successive governments into scaling up financial assistance.

The creation of the 'green' common market in 1962 was doubly beneficial to French agriculture, dramatically expanding its market base as well as the budget for financing price guarantees. The FEOGAs, set up to administer EC subsidies, extended their coverage from grain, pork, eggs and poultry (1962), to dairy products and beef (1963), sugar, fruit and vegetables, and oleaginous seeds (1966) and wine and tobacco (1970). As a consequence, French farm exports to the EC/EU jumped from 25 per cent of

Table 7.3 Total output by main crops, 1970–2000 (million tons or hectolitres)

Main products	1970	1980	1990	2000
Wheat	12.3	23.4	31.4	35.5
Maize	7.5	9.3	9.4	15.7
Beef	1.6	2.0	1.9	1.8
Pork	1.1	1.5	1.7	2.4
Milk	25.9	31.3	23.4	22.4
Cheese	0.7	1.2	1.5	1.5
Table wine	74.4	69.7	65.1	63.8
Quality wines	15.5	18.6	35.5	43.1

total French exports to 71 per cent in 1998. During the CAP's 'golden age', between 1962 and 1984 (when production caps were first introduced), French farmers enjoyed a period of considerable, albeit artificial, prosperity. As the unions[6] were prone to emphasise, French farmers had risen to the postwar challenge of providing the lifeblood of the nation: in 1946, each agriculturalist supplied, on average, food for 5.5 people; in 1975, for 26.

Meanwhile, as Cassandras had been predicting, the CAP was mechanically boosting the production of subsidised crops and bringing about ever-swelling surpluses which needed additional export subsidies enabling them to be dumped on foreign (extra-European) markets at competitive prices. French output and visible exports were still increasing but at an escalating cost to taxpayers. It was mainly in the production of standard staples that French achievements were the most spectacular: France became the fourth largest world producer of cereals and meat (Table 7.3). By contrast, France lagged behind in the production of more elaborate produce, such as fresh fruit and vegetables, as well as food processing.

As time went by the advantages of the CAP were gradually eroded by countervailing factors, some of them brought about by the very design of the scheme. It did not eliminate competition from outside the EC because the opening of borders diffused the effects of falling

---

[6] In the 1970s the CJA (Centre des Jeunes Agriculteurs) split from the main federation FNSEA. Always a minority group, it acquired fame recently thanks its his pugnacious leader, José Bové, hero of Seattle and Porto Alegre.

Table 7.4 CAP 'direct aid' subsidies by crop in 1999

	(billion francs)	%
Cereals	21.6	49.5
Oil seeds	8.0	18.3
Beef	7.5	17.2
Set-aside	2.8	6.4
Soya and feedstuffs	1.7	3.9
Mutton	1.4	3.2
Other	0.6	1.5
Total	43.6	100

prices. From 1984 onwards, the EC imposed caps on production and introduced mandatory set-aside of land, both of which were further extended in 1992. Meanwhile, farmers faced rising production costs which came to represent 70 per cent of the value of output, along with mounting financial costs (mortgage and loan repayments), the combined result of past (over)investment and the end of interest-rate-busting inflation. After a peak in 1973, farmers' incomes stagnated in the 1980s and declined further in the 1990s, alongside depreciation of their assets. In many peripheral regions farm buildings were abandoned for lack of incumbents and final emigration resumed with a vengeance. In 1996, the numbers employed in farming dropped under the one million mark (just above 4 per cent of the working population), half (57 per cent) of which were aged over fifty. The spectre of a vanishing farming sector, predicted by advocates of massive assistance since the 1960s, has finally become a reality. Under the circumstances, the majority of remaining French farmers have been becoming more dependent, not less, on government aid just as France's European partners (most recently through the reform put forward by EU Commissioner Franz Fischler) are pressing for a drastic reform of the CAP.

France figures with Spain and Ireland among the three major beneficiaries of the CAP and the 'direct aid' the latter provides represents on average between 25 and 30 per cent of farmers' annual income. This comes in addition to price support for specific crops. Together, they totalled around € 10 billion in 2000 and went predominantly to three standard staples: grain, oil seeds and beef. At one end of the spectrum, a quarter of all farms receive no CAP aid at all; at the other 20 per cent benefit from 62 per cent of CAP transfers (equivalent to £50,000 per farm per annum on average). A handful of large landowners, as an ecology minister imprudently revealed in 1999, enjoy annual handouts of upwards of a million francs (£100,000). In between, half of all farms receive the equivalent of £8,500 in aid, a sum which is barely sufficient to ensure their survival.

Government assistance is not limited to CAP subsidies. It can roughly be estimated that another € 10 billion is disbursed by the Treasury on behalf of farmers, not taking into account the budget of the Ministry of Agriculture, which itself employs a number of civil servants equivalent to that of the farm population! Consequently, public outlay on farming today is superior to its aggregate value added (€ 27.4 billion as against 23.9 billion). This has allowed France to remain at the top of the world charts for the production of basic foodstuffs (wheat, maize and beef) which are then dumped on extra-European markets with the help of export subsidies also provided by the CAP. Ironically, despite these enduring achievements the country still possesses a structural trade deficit in processed foods, and French food companies (IAAs) do not compare favourably in turnover, market power or profitability with their British or Swiss counterparts. Depicted as France's 'green oil' in the crude-oil-strapped 1970s, agriculture has turned out to be a form of 'green coal.[7]

[7] Coal-mining being another heavily subsidised industry in the EU.

Chapter 8
Industrialisation, de-industrialisation, postindustrialisation

By general European and world standards, French industrialisation started relatively early, France alongside Belgium and Switzerland being Britain's closest rival in the first half of the nineteenth century. However, as this survey has shown, the spread of industrial processes and the development of the secondary sector only really took hold after the First World War, and even more so after the Second. In 1970, France had become an industrial power, with 45 per cent of its GNP originating in the secondary sector. Within a decade, however, de-industrialisation had ushered in the virtual decimation of entire industries while service industries were, albeit imperfectly, taking their place.

Most French historians tend to treat the French 'path of development' as absolutely unique and are keen to vindicate the extensive government intervention which was supposedly deployed – in contrast to the British 'laissez-faire' model – to promote the country's industrial modernisation. On even a cursory inspection, however, the two paths appear remarkably similar if not parallel. Like Britain's (and those of most other developed countries), only with a varying time lag, France's economy went successively through the transformation of its agriculture and intensive industrialisation before shifting to sophisticated industrial operations and services. In the French case, the state is supposed to have played the decisive role in mobilising energies and encouraging technological innovation aimed at improving the wellbeing of the nation at large; but government intervention in industry for most of the twentieth century proved to be no less extensive in Britain than in France. However, deregulation, which sought to reverse some of the *dirigiste* policies adopted earlier and which Britain embraced in the 1980s, has been much slower to take hold across the Channel.

1. 'Restricted' industrialisation

Up to the Second World War, French industrialisation was limited in scope and incomplete by comparison with its immediate European competitors, Britain and Germany. The French network of industrial businesses as well as French industrial production were far from negligible, but the country's international position, in terms of both aggregate output and output per capita, had deteriorated since the middle of the nineteenth century when it was second only to Britain's. By 1930 (the second-best year of the interwar period), French industry had barely closed its productivity gap with Britain. With the new international leaders (USA, Germany), the gap was in fact widening.

Contemporary students of the French economy – 1930s reformers and postwar policy makers – were quick to assign the blame for this backwardness to 'Malthusian' forces which had hitherto acted as a brake on France's industrial development. Some of these constraints consisted of objective factors, such as a 'lack of minerals in the diet' (R. Cameron) – meaning inadequate coal reserves.[1] But, in contemporaries' view, most of the causes behind retardation were man-made. One was population stagnation,[2] which had negative implications for the rate of entry into the labour force as well as for saving and investment. But more important was the consensus established and reinforced in favour of the status quo: 'Stagnationists' especially targeted conservative industrialists for their lack of vision, poor entrepreneurship, aversion to innovation and risk and obsession with 'running their business like an annuity'.

The industrial workforce was remarkably stable between the turn of the twentieth century and the Second World War. In the aggregate, excluding mining and building (always subject to short-term variations), manufacturing industries employed about five million

---

[1] Although not as well endowed as Britain and Germany with metallic ores, France had substantial iron ore deposits (affectionately known as *minette*) in Lorraine.

[2] Alfred Sauvy (1902–90), the economist who coined the term 'Malthusianism' (implying voluntary restraint), started his career as a demographer.

Table 8.1 French labour productivity compared to British, 1906/7 and 1930/1

GB = 100	1906/7	1930/1
Mining	75.2	80.4
Basic metallurgy	85.8	81.0
Engineering	84.4	89.1
Non-ferrous metals	86.1	88.8
Chemicals	74.2	60.6
Textiles	73.6	78.0
Clothing	79.4	94.3
Leather	72.2	60.4
Paper	78.9	62.7
Food and drink	54.0	62.2
Wood and furniture	72.2	81.9
Building materials	67.1	68.1
Public utilities	82.1	67.1
Building and construction	81.2	74.1
Average	**74.5**	**77.6**

people in 1906, just as they did in 1936 (in about a quarter of a million plants). Although 'putting out' (industrial work done in the home) had virtually disappeared and establishments with fewer than five workers employed only 20 per cent of the total labour force, three quarters of all factories were still devoid of motive power and most concerns (essentially workshops) operated on a small scale. A handful of factories employed 1,000 workers or more, in collieries, iron foundries and textile mills. Industrial activity encompassed three types of firms and production. First, the rank and file was made up of firms producing consumer goods for local, regional and sometimes national markets. Production was typically small scale and 'customised'. Secondly, a small group of dynamic, specialised industries manufactured luxury or otherwise sophisticated goods for the narrow and distinctive upper end of domestic and international markets. Thirdly, large, capital-intensive units produced intermediate and semi-finished goods such as fuel, metals and textile fabrics destined to be dispatched (or exported) for further processing in smaller, specialised industries. By the end of the

Table 8.2 Distribution of French firms by size of payroll, 1906–66 (% of total)

No. of employees	1906	1931	1954	1966
1 to 10	32.2	19.7	16.2	13.1
11 to 100	27.6	30.1	30.8	31.9
101 to 500	21.7	23.6	25.9	29.0
500 and over	18.5	26.6	27.1	26.0
Employees (thsds)	3679	5442	5918	6831

1920s, French industry, after recouping its wartime losses, went through a brisk boom which saw a spate of mergers. The distribution of industrial employment then remained remarkably stable until the late 1960s. Stagnation in the 1930s and during the Second World War swept aside most of the gains in output and performance obtained in the 1920s: by 1948 the value of French industrial output was only 10 per cent above the 1913 level, implying an annual growth rate of only 0.5 per cent over a thirty-five-year period.

2. An 'imperious necessity'

The wind of change which blew over the country at the time of its liberation (1944–5) called on decision makers in government and business to discard the old forms of paternalistic and corporatist capitalism.

To regain its standing among modern Western economies, it was imperative that France should build up and modernise its industrial structure. The consensus embraced the whole political spectrum, from General de Gaulle and his cross-party following to Maurice Thorez, the Communist leader who called on his comrades to 'work, work and work'.[3] The first challenge was to rebuild the country's badly damaged infrastructure and boost the production of collective goods (energy, transport). This ambitious programme, first sketched by the CNR, was set out by Jean Monnet at the head of the CGP in the first five-year plan in 1946 – taking on board proposals

---

[3] From his speech at the Waziers collieries on 21 July 1945.

Table 8.3 Sectoral and economy-wide annual growth rates, 1905–75 (%)

	Agriculture	Industry	Services	GDP
1905–13	0.69	2.02	1.45	1.51
1920–4	0.10	1.35	1.11	1.04
1925–34	1.48	4.38	2.35	3.07
1935–8	0.43	0.24	0.16	0.30
1949–55	1.21	2.58	1.85	2.10
1956–60	1.73	5.56	4.36	4.62
1961–5	3.34	6.90	4.61	5.46
1966–70	1.93	6.95	4.44	5.33
1970–5	1.31	5.85	4.95	5.18

made by Vichy officials. To ensure adequate deliveries (as well as ensure a fair distribution of its benefits to the nation at large) the government assumed responsibility for the management of key industries by nationalising a number of large concerns (see Chapter 4). The Marshall Plan provided the pump-priming ($ 4.6 billion) to revive production in key sectors, which soon attained healthy growth rates before soaring to unimaginable heights in the next twenty years (just short of 7 per cent in the 1960s). Visibly, after 1950, industry was becoming a powerful engine of French economic growth (Table 8.3).

Historians have usually been inclined to echo the triumphalism implicit or explicit in the macroeconomic accounts of the period published by officials and economists (Margairaz, 1991); they have tended moreover to give credit to government economic and industrial policies for these achievements. With hindsight, however, the direction taken by France during its 'great leap forward' in industrialisation contained the seeds of future trouble. The emphasis was placed first on intermediary and collective goods, and secondly on semi-durables rather than consumption goods. This orientation was in fact best suited to French capabilities at the time, in terms of fixed and human capital endowment as well as of available technology and productive organisation.

While overall capital formation gradually improved in the postwar period, eventually rising to 26 per cent of GDP in 1970 (the

1929 record of 20 per cent was not broken untill 1960), industrial investment represented only a fraction of this total, edging up to 6 per cent during the 'Golden Age'. Manufacturers still relied predominantly on the prewar common practice of ploughing back (reinvesting) profits – a policy which both made company boards less dependent on the stock market (unlike the issue of new equity) and preserved the independence of the management vis-à-vis the shareholders. Securitisation remained accordingly limited: the total amount of securities hovered around 2 per cent of GDP between 1954 and 1970.

The issue of new equity and credit allowances, carefully monitored by the Treasury, benefited primarily GENs (large SOEs) and large private concerns with government contracts or captive markets. During this period, cross-financing created a complicated but self-contained maze of financial holdings between major private and public firms. Meanwhile, with limited access to capital markets, the indebtedness of other firms (those most exposed to market competition) tended to deteriorate over the long term, especially during economic downturns. Furthermore, the build-up of 'national champions' (with privileged access to markets) in energy and public utilities, in capital equipment (vehicles, aircraft, shipbuilding), and in intermediary goods (steel, basic chemicals) suited the prevailing conditions as regarded the supply of skills (R&D played a marginal role in industries with mature or stable technologies). These were highly centralised businesses with design and chain management entrusted to an elite of managers and engineers while shopfloor operations were handled by unskilled operatives (OS). The latter comprised the two million workers who had only just transferred from the farm or the shop, along with the existing industrial workforce.

Finally, inasmuch as economies of scale were thought to be the high road to centralised production, the recommendations of F. W. Taylor and Henry Ford half a century earlier (the assembly line and automated production) were considered as the best way to implement mass production of standardised goods. Thus, France's economic path of development during the 'Golden Age' was implicitly intended to accommodate and preserve a certain power structure. In this sense, it can be argued that both the 'liberal capitalist' economies of the West and those of the Soviet bloc pursued in this period a model of development which sought

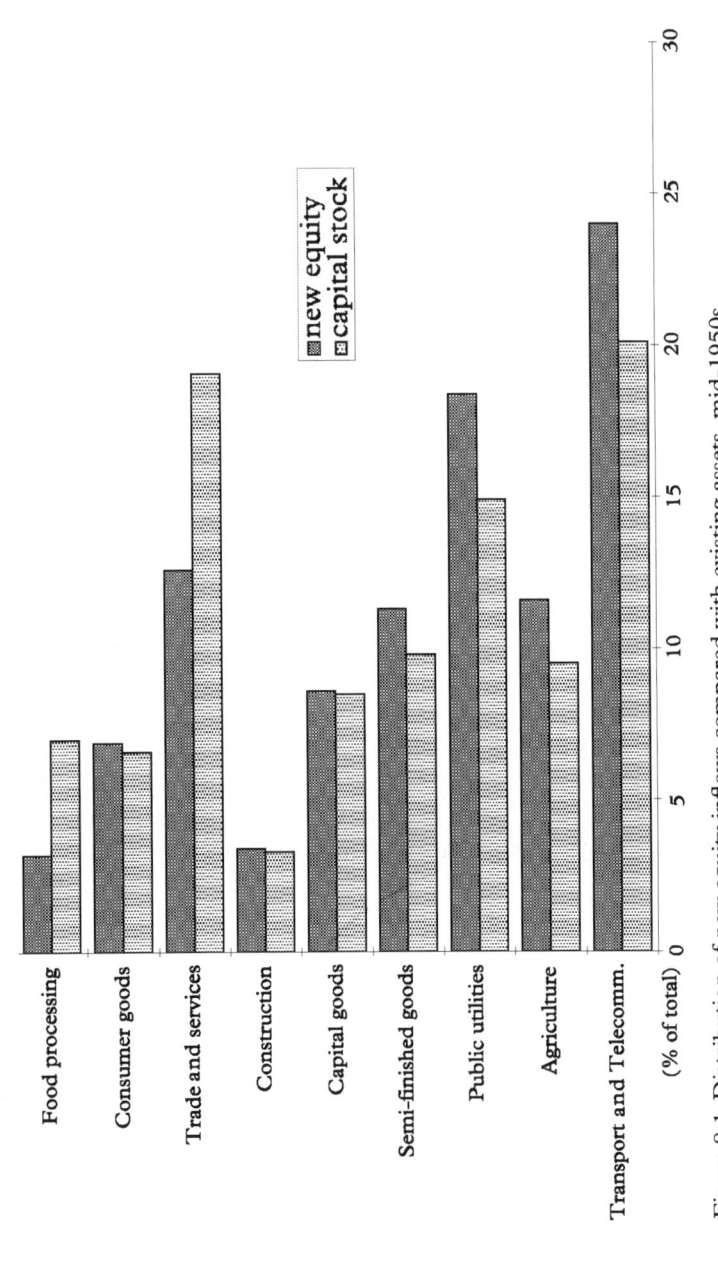

Figure 8.1 Distribution of new equity inflows compared with existing assets, mid-1950s

Table 8.4 Changes in manufacturing employment by sectors, 1960–2000

(thsds)	1960	1974	1980	2000
Intermediate goods	1441	1740	1521	1431
Equipment goods	1023	1407	1297	778
Vehicles	310	489	509	246
Consumer goods	1709	1610	1450	1321
Total	4483	5246	4777	3776

to favour the satisfaction of collective needs and check private consumption accordingly. EDF's tariff implicitly advantaged corporate consumers over individual private ones: two major firms (Wendel-Sidelor and Usinor) monopolised the production of steel under the cover of the ECSC cartel arrangement; the pharmaceutical industry expanded under the shelter of official regulations and thanks also to social security funding; aircraft and shipbuilding, as well as electrical engineering, were largely dependent on government procurement or subsidies; import quotas reserved the domestic market to French-made cars and home appliances. By comparison, consumer goods industries fared less well (dropping from 10.5 per cent to 8.8 per cent of aggregate value added between 1952 and 1972), and they did not keep pace with domestic demand sustained by rising disposable incomes generated in the rest of the economy, which necessarily fuelled an increase in manufactured imports. Starved of investment and reluctant to innovate, these industries had relied since the interwar period on exports to captive markets (in the colonial empire) which evaporated as a result of decolonisation (1954–62), the industrialisation of former overseas territories, and their capture by foreign competitors. Typical of this type was the textile industry, which went through a long period of decline before collapsing in the 1980s.

French industry (including mining and construction) registered its all-time peak of employment in 1974, when it employed 8.3 million workers representing 38.5 per cent of total employment. The oil crisis of 1973–9 ushered in a period of drastic reduction in productive capacity. Over the eight years until 1982 all the major

Table 8.5 Foreign trade in manufactures, 1974–2000 (*billion francs*)

(1995 prices)	1974	1990	2000
Exports	598	1027	1944
Imports	561	1090	2005
Coverage	106%	94%	97%

industries shed labour and contracted their payrolls. Employment fell by 80,000 in steel-making, by 176,000 in textiles, and by 25,000 in shipbuilding. This destruction of jobs encouraged the Socialist government's decision to nationalise nine major industrial groups (employing a total of 0.9 million workers) in 1982 in a bid to stop the haemorrhage. However, such a stance quickly proved untenable in the following years and it was reversed by major downsizing operations in 1984–5 before successive governments gradually returned most enterprises to the private sector.

Whilst industrial activities contracted between 1974 and 1998 from 38 to 23 per cent of the workforce, France's foreign trade in manufactures continued to expand. In spite of this, however, its international position deteriorated, as it slipped into the position of a net importer of manufactured goods. The resulting deficit is now covered by sales of 'invisible' services.

3. The 'invisibles revolution'

The contribution of the tertiary sector (services or 'invisibles') to GNP first equalled that of industry (the secondary sector) in 1931[4] and surpassed it continuously after 1945. During the postwar period, the tertiary sector absorbed a comparatively greater share of new labour market entrants so that by 1974 it employed one out of every two workers. For a few years in the mid-1990s, France even overtook Japan and Germany as the second major exporter of services. By 2000, the share of the tertiary sector was so overwhelming (comparable to that of Britain and Germany) that it became

---

[4] That same year, according to the population census (5 March, 1931) the proportion of urban dwellers overtook the rural population.

Table 8.6 Sectoral and economy-wide labour productivity 1901–38 (indexed on 1901 in constant francs)

	Agriculture	Industry	Services	Economy-wide
1901	67	120	99	100
1911	69	142	118	118
1921	70	154	130	112
1931	108	215	211	176
1938	86	187	167	144

obvious that services were playing (and had done for some time) a leading role in domestic wealth creation. Until recently, however, French historians have devoted scant attention to this process and have tended to cling to an 'industrialist' vision of economic development.

As in other countries at comparable stages of development, the growth of the business service sector after 1900 has been propelled by two forces: the 'widening' and 'deepening' of industrialisation. Industrial firms progressively farmed out previously internal functions (upstream and downstream of 'throughput' proper) such as conception, design, accounting, advertising and marketing. For personal services, a shift in consumer preferences away from physical goods boosted the provision of welfare enhancing services.[5] Additions to the service sector were incremental up to the mid-century (7.2 million in 1950 compared to 5.5 million in 1906), but it more than doubled in size in the second half of the century (to 15.7 million or 69.5 per cent of total employment).

Up to the Second World War, the existence of a relatively underdeveloped tertiary sector reflected a lack of dynamism in the industrial, urban economy. Small family-run manufacturing businesses (the majority) tended to rely on their own resources (as they did for investment), reinforced by the relatively low standard of living of potential customers still predominantly living in villages and small towns. Rural communities also preferred self-sufficiency and were

---

[5] Oxford's Avner Offer calls the first 'visceral goods' and the second 'prudential goods'.

suspicious of uncalled-for innovations: 'demand was typically weak, costs were high and productivity low' (P. K. O' Brien). Personal services such as medical care constitute a prime example, despite publicity attending on the prestige of such practitioners as Louis Pasteur (1822–95). *Knock* (a foreign-sounding name, in the xenophobia-prone interwar period), an eponymous popular play written in 1923 by Jules Romains, describes arduous canvassing by a dynamic physician, newly arrived in a provincial town and anxious to increase his practice.

Before 1914 productivity in services was probably lower than in the economy as a whole (see Table 8.6), but this average summed up a variety of situations. The service sector as a whole can be roughly mapped according to dominant forms of organisation:

	+ traditional −	− modernised +
corporate services	legal practice transport expert services distribution	financial communications
personal services	retail trade medical services education domestic service civil service	hotels public services

Relatively low overall performance (by comparison with that registered in Britain, the USA or Germany) can be accounted for by the small size and traditional organisation of concerns more or less concentrating on any one activity, as well as by their degree of competitiveness. Not being the subject of international exchange, service 'industries' were usually less receptive to market pressure to adopt competitive organisation and modes of production. As a consequence most branches of services tended to display a mixture of 'modern' and 'traditional' firms. This was particularly the case in transport, where French rail companies could compete with foreign competitors in terms of efficiency and profitability, whereas the performance of the transport sector as a whole was weighed down by low returns on traditional modes of conveyance. A second group was made up of activities which had maintained a customary organisation and/or enjoyed privileged status. Some were the direct heirs to the guilds of the Ancien Régime. This was the case for most of the 'liberal' (or learned) professions which had their respective monopolies guaranteed by statute. At the other end of the social hierarchy, domestic service (still employing 750,000 persons in 1938) served predominantly as a transit route for rural migrants to more rewarding positions in the urban economy. Retail trade was still massively organised along traditional lines: one and a half million outlets – their numbers increased between the wars – were scattered across the country. Despite the early opening of department stores in Paris under the Second Empire, economies of scale were necessarily limited due to the dispersion of the population. Regional chain stores started to spread (Docks Rémois, Casino, Familistère) after 1900, mainly in provincial centres of industry and usually as outgrowths from of purchasing co-ops. Monoprix, a chain store, introduced uniform pricing in 1928. As in the case of family farms, the Third Republic was intent on preserving traditional distribution patterns; post-First-World-War tax legislation introduced in 1917 and 1928 (see Chapter 4) was aimed at preserving small units in retail trade.[6]

A number of French firms, however, offered world-class services. This was especially the case in financial services, catering and communications. Before the first war, Paris was a preferred location for the headquarters of prestigious private banking establishments, a central bank which ranked on a par with the Bank of England and an active stock exchange. But French banks were badly hit by the post-1917 Russian default on government and other bonds. The considerable loss of assets during the war was compounded by inflation (Schuker, 1976).

The post-1945 'service revolution' was a critical ingredient of the French 'economic miracle'. Industrial expansion, especially after the mid-1950s, was accompanied by the development of large

---

[6] Large concerns were taxed on the basis of turnover; shopkeepers with concerns below a certain size could opt freely for the tax bracket they thought applied to their business.

swathes of the service sector where employment grew in the aggregate faster and more steadily than in manufacturing. The service sector recorded its fastest growth between 1963 and 1973. By the time of the 1973 oil crisis it had become the leading sector of the French economy. Its foreign trade balance improved constantly from 5.3 billion francs in 1973 to upwards of 45 billion in 1989 and beyond.

During the last two decades of the century, service industries provided the backbone of the French economic recovery: their workforce increased by a quarter. This has affected proportionately more tradeable services (excluding trade and distribution which have remained stable) than non-tradeable services (most of them supplied by the state). Twelve of the country's thirty largest firms today are service providers (there were ony four in 1960), including former government monopolies: the rail operator SNCF, Air France, La Poste and France Telecom. Before he had to resign in 2002 amidst accusations of impropriety, Jean-Marie Messier, the controversial tycoon, turned his company Vivendi (formerly Générale des Eaux) into a huge conglomerate, dealing in everything from piped water to movies and mobile phones, and with sizeable shares in world markets.

While the most publicised ventures typically associate service provision with manufacturing expertise (for example the Ariane space shuttle), French retailers have managed to effect a complete transformation of their industry. The spread of supermarkets was kept in check until the 1960s, when a group of early entrants (among them Carrefour and Casino) had gained influence over planning committees.[7] Within ten years Edouard Leclerc, originally a shopkeeper in Landernau (Brittany), managed to break the cosy oligopoly of his competitors by setting up his own brand of supermarkets inside his home region and then throughout France. After relying on high street shops for three generations, turn of the century French people now visit shopping malls in droves, pushing retail turnover and profits ever higher: super- and hypermarkets (those larger than 2,500 square metres) now supply 62 and 35 per cent respectively of all

---

[7] The loi Royer of 1973 imposed tougher restrictions on the establishment of large shopping areas.

food and non-food items. Together, Carrefour, Intermarché and a later entrant, Auchan (the property of the Bettencourt family, the richest in the land), have stakes in or control 189 store chains abroad. Former public operators, such as France Telecom and the postal service – now rebranded under the name of 'La Poste',[8] have been much less successful in penetrating foreign markets.

Tourism, film making and music recording have all overtaken former flagship industries like steel-making in their contribution to GDP. Tourism in particular contributes significantly to the balance of payments. By 2000, seventy million foreign visitors (excluding immigrants) were flocking annually to France, which now holds the world record for inward tourism. Club Med (holiday packages), created by Gilbert Trigano in 1950, remains unparallelled in its category. AXA, an insurer, grew out of a small mutual fund in Normandy to become the first French company listed (45th) among the hundred leading world firms. Prestigious American law firms and international publicity agencies, as well as home-grown competitors such as Havas (established in 1832) and Publicis (1926), have set up shop in fashionable districts of Paris.

With the development of its service economy, France has undoubtedy been able to capitalise on long-standing but hitherto untapped marketing capabilities. Like industry in the first stages of industrialisation, however, the tertiary transformation of the economy looks daunting to most people who find themselves subjected to its demands for adaptability and flexibility. This atmosphere contributes to a feeling of unease about the sustainability of French living standards, already slipping behind those of the rest of northern Europe. Besides, the most promising avenues of export earnings, profits and ultimately employment rest with services geared to improving the provision of physical goods. The systematic delocalisation of assembly lines to allegedly more favourable climes naturally arouses legitimate worries about the sustainability of such an arrangement. In addition, it tends to write off that section of the labour force with skills or tastes more suited to manual work. Perhaps this can be altered, but only, it seems, by an overhaul of

---

[8] The state still retains a 'golden share' (51%) in France Telecom's stock which was partially privatised in 1998; in La Poste it is the sole shareholder.

Table 8.7 Employment, value added and labour productivity across the economy, 2000

	Employment (% of total)	Value added (% of total)	Productivity Index
Agriculture, fisheries, forestry	**4.3**	**2.8**	**68**
Industry	**22.7**	**25.4**	**158**
Food processing	2.5	2.6	107
Consumer goods	3.0	3.1	106
Vehicles	1.0	1.5	150
Capital goods	3.2	3.5	112
Semi-finished goods	5.9	6.8	117
Energy	0.9	3.4	386
Construction	6.2	4.5	76
Private services	**45.1**	**51.6**	**118**
Trade	13.8	10.0	75
Transport	4.6	4.0	90
Financial services	3.1	4.7	154
Real estate	1.6	12.2	789
Professional services	13.4	15.0	116
Personal services	8.6	5.7	68
Public services	**27.9**	**20.2**	**74**
Education, health, social services	15.6	11.4	75
Administration	12.3	8.7	73
Economy	100 or 24.1m	100 or €1288bn	100 or €51,900

the extensive redistribution system developed since 1945. Today, cross-subsidisation makes it very difficult to distinguish between really productive activities and others which could not subsist in the absence of direct and indirect transfers generated by the welfare state and government industrial policy in its various guises. Even labour productivity indicators (in the absence of information about market distortions and direct or indirect support) are poor guides to distinguishing one from the other. They suggest, however, that France's strength remains with its now cut-down-to-size manufacturing sector, the most open to outside competition, and the best performing of its services, such as finance and the professions.

Others seem to constitute a drag rather a boost to the country's overall wealth-generating capacity: Airbus, Bull, Air France, Crédit Lyonnais and the rest still have to prove that they can turn out regular profits. The way ahead is clearly to further open services to international competition, in which France is well equipped to score further points.

Conclusion

> The French want no one to be their superior. The English want inferiors.
> The Frenchman constantly raises his eyes above him with anxiety. The Englishman lowers his beneath him with satisfaction.
>
> Alexis de Tocqueville, *Voyage en Angleterre et en Irlande de 1835*

Like other very self-conscious nations, the French tend to view their past as an epic and read the twentieth century as the progress of their nation towards the realisation of a more perfect model. In most accounts of French economic history, the country's achievements tend to be assessed in a purely national framework, in the light not so much of comparable economies as of its own past achievements or else assessed in the light of moral values or expectations. The notion inherited from nineteenth-century geographers, that the French territory seen from on high espouses the ideal shape of a 'hexagon', suggests that, as General de Gaulle expressed it, the fate of the nation could not be equated with or reduced to the vicissitudes of its people.

Hence the tendency among historians of the French economy to study economic objects, such as firms, over the long term, or else to overemphasise political factors in short-term economic developments, while ignoring blatant cross-border similarities. With hindsight, the national economy of the second half of the century was markedly different from what it had been in the first. Most authors, however, are keen to stress the progressivity of 'modernisation' and detect in the first the seeds of change that did not materialise until later. Business history, the main branch of the discipline of economic history as practised in France, has reinforced this tendency. Certainly the early twenty-first century economy retains features reminiscent of its distant predecessor of a century earlier: ageism, then as now, threatens France's economic dynamism; the country's total working population in 2000 (in absolute numbers) was only 10% higher than in 1900. Of course, the composition of economic activities has changed dramatically, but today's French society is still heavily skewed towards inactivity and leisure: only 37.3 per cent of the total population is actually in employment, the lowest in the fifteen countries of the EU (49.4 per cent in the UK, 48.6 per cent in Germany, 40.5 per cent in Italy).

In 2000, as in 1900, a number of privileged activities benefited from government protection and support, including agriculture and a host of public services: today's prevalent egalitarianism, like that of the Belle Epoque, remains suspicious of the market economy, but taxpayers are increasingly unwilling to bear the cost of a redistributive machinery which has become harder and harder to maintain. Shorn of large emigrant communities overseas (if one excepts the five million temporary expatriates), the French are wary of outside influence and tend to perceive the outside world as hostile to French interests and culture. Hence the popularity throughout the twentieth century of anti-globalisation movements under their various guises.

For the past thirty years, to a large extent France has sought to evade rather than to confront the challenges of the global economy as most of its neighbours and economic partners have done. High unemployment and gradual demotion in terms of per capita income have been the price France has had to pay for this procrastination. The French, once among the keenest supporters of European integration, are now the slowest nation but one when it comes to aligning legislation on European directives.

Being at the crossroads between northern and Mediterranean Europe, the country has always naturally borrowed cultural features from these two blocks. In the first half of the twentieth century (continuing a powerful trend of the nineteenth) it tended to gravitate towards liberal and constitutional Britain. After the Second World War, though drawn economically towards a 'Rhineland' model of the 'social market economy' (Albert, 1991) and a German political alliance, France has reinforced its resemblances to its 'Latin sister', Italy. Waves of migrants from southern Europe (Spain, Italy, Portugal) and, more recently, from North Africa (including *pieds noirs** of

Italian and Spanish descent from Tunisia and Algeria) have tilted the ethnic balance towards the Mediterranean element in the French population. Moreover the path of development followed by Italy and France since the wars (during which both countries reversed alliances) has been remarkably similar: they have recently added to their traditional strong points – luxuries, designer fashions, wines and spirits – advances in durables and equipment goods. By 2000 Italy's industrial output was poised to overtake its French counterpart in aggregate value added, while the two countries retain a vested interest in the CAP to sustain the remnants of their farming sector. And both countries present widening regional inequality between privileged, economically active areas and impoverished, backward areas.

In France, carefully maintained historical sites and skilfully advertised, well-manicured market towns and villages, which call forth the admiration of foreign tourists, conceal a growing economic and social divide between the dynamic and congested business centres and the vast expanse of a 'mezzogiorno in the making' which includes large tracts of the interior and south-west, between leafy residential suburbs and classy city centres on the one hand and dreary, dilapidated *cités** on the other.

Long-time laggards in terms of modern infrastructure, both France and Italy today boast (and owe part of their prosperity to) successful capitalist enterprises (the most popular French and Italian brands abroad are invariably fashion items); public opinion by and large, however, remains distrustful of capitalism and the free market. While people may grumble against the bureaucracy, they still accept, sometimes cynically, the need for extensive government intervention and the maintenance of an extensive public sector. In both countries a host of well-organised interest groups can mobilise to protect their own interests and are even in a position to hold the country to ransom. Large swathes of the population[1] in the two countries are hostile to free-market reform and envision social progress solely in terms of the repression of market forces and bringing the private sector in line with public sector

---

[1] In France it can be roughly estimated at close to half of the adult population or 22 million, including public servants, pensioners, and persons who are unemployed, supported by the RMI or on various job support schemes, as well as students in further education.

practice (job protection law, minimum wage, automatic promotion according to seniority, statutory pension benefits etc.). As a result, while the cost of the welfare state has escalated to ever higher levels, the underground economy has flourished in France, where it may yet come to equal Italy's. In this respect, economic illiteracy and the endurance of unorthodox doctrines in academic teaching[2] and the media contribute to keeping radical utopias on the political agenda.[3] Meanwhile, this belief may encourage dependency, or encourage special arrangements – *débrouillardise* ('smartness') or *combinazione* (implying job rigging, corruption and graft) – justified by the need to curb market forces in order to protect the weak and the powerless, a strategy which usually only leads to a strengthening of vested interests, that is, of the powerful.

More tragically, this turn of events has contributed to weakening the work ethic and encouraging escapism (witness the consumption of sleeping pills and the suicide rate); the French are thus increasingly led to envision gainful employment (or *travail*) as an arduous necessity, even a curse, and not as a career offering opportunities to expand their capabilities as well as their living standards. The aspiration to a life of leisure, already noted by Friedrich Sieburg in the 1920s and boosted by the *soixante-huitard** claim of a 'right to idleness', is pervasive throughout French society, especially among the young. As a result, the ongoing demotion of the French economy, reminiscent of similar episodes at the turn of the century and during the interwar years (Kemp, 1972), may have more profound causes than simply economic anaemia or international competition.

---

[2] The 'regulation school' can be aptly viewed as rebranded Marxism (the labour theory of value) tinged with Keynesianism (structural pump-priming policies).
[3] France, like Italy, boasts an unreformed Communist party with representation in Parliament, as well as a sizeable far-right without parliamentary representation in France.

Glossary

Accords de Grenelle: June 1968 tripartite (unions-employers-government) agreement on pay and working conditions which ended the May strikes and riots
Accords Matignon: June 1936 tripartite agreement on pay and working conditions following the electoral victory of the Popular Front
atelier: industrial workshop, usually of small size
baccalauréat: secondary education diploma
Banque de France: France's central bank (est. 1800)
beur: second-generation Arab immigrants (inverted from 'arabe'; pun on 'butter')
cadres: (production) managers
Cartel des Gauches: Electoral alliance enabling coalition government by Radicals and Socialists (1924)
certificat d'études: primary education diploma
cité: suburban housing estate
cohabitation: situation in which the head of state and the prime minister are of opposing political parties
comités d'entreprise: works councils (est. 1945)
commune: basic administrative division of territory (roughly equivalent to a borough)
conseil des prud'hommes: industrial tribunal (est. 1848)
corps intermédiaires: non-political representative organisations
département: administrative territorial division corresponding to an English county
député: member of the French legislature
Deux Cents Familles: France's richest families with one or more members on the board of regents of the Banque de France (until 1937)
dirigisme: the managed economy in doctrine and practice
droits acquis: social and economic entitlements
école normale: teacher training college
fabrique: industrial establishment

Glossary 133

fonctionnaire: government employee or civil servant
fonction publique: public or civil service
franc zone: postwar monetary union between France and its present and former overseas possessions using the franc as a common currency
Front Populaire: Electoral alliance between and government of Radicals, Socialists and Communists (1936)
grands corps (de l'Etat): prestigious government departments or agencies
grandes écoles: elite higher education institutions with competitive admission
Latin Quarter: the Paris district including the university of the Sorbonne; place of student uprising in May 1968
Liberation: i.e. from Nazi occupation; by extension, the period from 6 June, 1944 to 16 January, 1946, when General de Gaulle resigned the premiership
loi: an act passed by the French Parliament, usually bearing the name of its promoter
lotissement: suburban residential estate
Métropolitain (in short **Métro**): undergound suburban railway
mur de l'argent: a phrase used to denounce the opposition of business interests to inflationary policies in the interwar period
Nouvelle Vague ('new wave'): a school of naturalist film-making at the turn of the 1960s
OPA: (company) take-over
organisations syndicales représentatives: officially recognised labour organisations
pantouflage: transfer of higher civil servants on to company boards
paritarisme: statutory, tripartite association of government, employers' and union representatives in settling industrial disputes
pieds noirs: French colonists and their descendants resettled in France from North Africa after 1962
pistonner (coll.): to pull strings for someone; to job-rig
plan de relance: pump-priming policy: demand is boosted by government expenditure so as to stimulate the economy
plan de rigueur: policy geared to restore public finances and slow down economic activity
préfet (prefect): central government chief executive in a *département*
rentier: person of private means; (government) bond holder (fixed annuity), hence, timid investor
soixante-huitard: 'veteran' of the May 1968 student uprising; anti-capitalist, left-wing ideology
taxe professionnelle: corporation tax levied to finance technical training
technocrate: higher civil servant or decision-maker with a scientific training
tribunal de commerce: commercial and bankruptcy court

A national portrait gallery of twentieth-century France

Allais, Maurice (b. 1911): France's only Nobel laureate in economics (1988)
Armand, Louis (1905–71): Charismatic first CEO of the rail utility SNCF
Aron, Raymond (1905–83): Philosopher and sociologist; anti-totalitarian activist
Aubry, Martine (b. 1940): Daughter of Jacques Delors; minister and sponsor of the thirty-five-hour week
Auriol, Vincent (1884–1966): Finance minister of the Popular Front 1936–7; first President of the Fourth Republic, 1946
Bachelard, Gaston (1884–1962): Philosopher, author of *Le Nouvel Esprit Scientifique* (1934)
Bardot, Brigitte (b. 1934): Movie star and leading figure of the *Nouvelle Vague**
Barre, Raymond (b. 1924): Vice president of the EEC Commission; French PM 1976–81
Baudrier, Jacqueline (b. 1922): Last head of monopoly broadcaster Radio France (1975–81)
Baumgartner, Wilfrid (1902–78): Head of the Banque de France 1949–60; minister of finance 1960–2
de Beauvoir, Simone (1908–86): Philosopher and feminist author of *The Second Sex* (1949)
Bérégovoy, Pierre (1925–93): Chief of staff to François Mitterrand 1981; PM 1992–93
Bettencourt, Liliane (date of birth unknown): Daughter of André Bettencourt; head of L'Oréal and the Auchan supermarket chain.
Beuve-Méry, Hubert (1902–89): Founder and first director of *Le Monde* newspaper, 1944
Bichelonne, Jean (1904–44): Industry minister in Vichy government
Bienvenüe, Fulgence (1852–1936): Planner and architect of Paris underground (*Métro*)

A national portrait gallery of twentieth-century France   135

Blériot, Louis (1872–1936): Flight pioneer; first to fly across the English Channel, 1909
Bleustein-Blanchet, Marcel (1906–96): Founder of Publicis, advertiser and pioneer of radio advertising, 1929
Bloch, Marc (1886–1944): Historian, co-founder with Lucien **Febvre** of the *Annales* school
Bloch Lainé, François (b. 1912): Head of the Treasury (1947–52), CDC and Banque de France*; presided over re-establishment of the franc
Blum, Léon (1872–1950): Socialist leader and PM of Popular Front, 1936
Bonnet, Georges (1889–1973): Farm minister and creator of ONIB (1936); appeasement-inclined foreign minister in 1938–40
Bourgeois, Léon (1851–1925): Radical party theorist and PM 1902–6
Bouthillier, Yves (1901–77): Finance secretary in the Pétain administration (1940–44)
Bouygues, Francis (1922–93): Founder of Bouygues, a major construction firm (1952)
Briand, Aristide (1862–1932): Six times PM before 1930; architect of reconciliation with Germany, 1926–9
Caillaux, Joseph (1863–1944): Finance minister who introduced the income tax in 1914
Cannac, Yves (b. 1935): Chief of staff to Giscard d'Estaing; head of Havas publicity agency
Carné, Marcel (1906–96): Emblematic film director
Ceyrac, François (b. 1912): Long-serving head of the employers' association CNPF
Chaban-Delmas, Jacques (1915–2000): PM 1969–72 and Mayor of Bordeaux
Chanel, Coco (Gabrielle Bonheur, 1883–1951): Top designer and creator of firm of same name
Chautemps, Camille (1885–1963): Several times PM in 1930s; supporter of immobilist and appeasement policy
Chirac, Jacques (b. 1932): PM 1974–6 and 1986–8; president of the Republic since 1995
Chotard, Yvon (1921–98): President of CNPF 1986; negotiator of Accords Matignon*
Citroën, André (1878–1935): Founder and CEO of motor manufacturing firm of same name
Clémenceau, Georges (1841–1929): Nicknamed 'the tiger'; founder of the Republican party; 'France's first cop' before the First World War and forceful wartime PM 1917–20
Clémentel, Etienne (1864–1936): Trade and industry secretary during the First World War
Combes, Emile (1835–1921): PM 1902–5 and leader in the fight against the Catholic church

Cot, Pierre (1911–93): Air minister under the Popular Front who boosted aircraft production before the Second World War

Cotta, Michèle (b. 1937): Head of Radio France 1981–85; supervised liberalisation of the airwaves

Cresson, Edith (b. 1934): Mitterrand favourite, short-lived PM 1991–2 and failed EU commissioner

Curie, Marie (1867–1934): Pioneer radium physicist and Nobel prize laureate in both physics and chemistry

Darcy, Henry (1840–1926) first and forceful president of the CGPF

Dassault, Marcel (1892–1986): Pioneer aircraft manufacturer

Debré, Michel (1912–96): First PM of the Fifth Republic, 1959–62

Defferre, Gaston (1911–86): Long-time mayor of Marseilles; interior minister and initiator of devolution to *départements** and regions in 1982

Delors, Jacques (b. 1935): Finance minister 1981–3 and President of the EC Commission

Dior, Christian (1905–57): Designer and creator of haute couture firm of same name

Doisneau, Robert (1912–94): Emblematic photographer of *Trente Glorieuses**

Dorgères, Roland (1897–1965): Farmers' unionist, founder of the *Comités de Défense Paysanne*, 1928

Duclos, Jacques (1896–1975): *De facto* head of Communist party in the 1960s

Eiffel, Gustave (1832–1923): Construction engineer and architect of the Eiffel tower

Fabius, Laurent (b. 1946): France's youngest PM of the twentieth century, 1984–6

Faure, Edgar (1908–88): Left-of-centre PM (1955) and several times minister under the Fourth Republic; sponsor of large-scale post-1968 education reform

Flandin, Pierre-Etienne (1889–1958): PM 1934–5 and minister in Pétain's government, 1940

Foch, Ferdinand (1851–1929): Commander-in-chief of Allied armies in 1918

Fouchet, Christian (1911–74): Education minister in 1960s; mishandled 1968 student uprising

Frachon, Benoît (1893–1975): General secretary of CGT trade union

Gabin, Jean (Jean Moncorgé, 1904–76): Emblematic film actor from the 1930s to the 1960s

Gallimard, Gaston (1881–1975): Founder and head of up-market publishing firm of the same name

de Gaulle, Charles (1890–1970): Free French leader in the Second World War; head of government 1944–6; President of the Republic 1958–69

A national portrait gallery of twentieth-century France 137

Gingembre, Léon (1904–1993): Founder and president of the CGPME
Giroud, Françoise (1916–2002): French journalist and politician, founder of *Elle* and *L'Express* magazines
Giscard d'Estaing, Valéry (b. 1926): Finance minister 1962–68; President of the Republic 1974–81
Haberer, Jean-Yves (b. 1932): Head of Treasury and controversial CEO of Crédit Lyonnais
Haby, René (b. 1919): Education minister 1974–8 and author of controversial reform (comprehensive schools)
Hanau, Marthe (1886–1937): Controversial stock-market maverick and financial publisher
Herriot, Edouard (1872–1957): Head of Radical party; PM under Cartel des Gauches* 1924–6; President of National Assembly 1936–40; long-serving Mayor of Lyons
Jaurès, Jean (1859–1914): Socialist leader and editor of *L'Humanité* (est. 1904)
Jeanneney, Jean-Marcel (b. 1910): Minister of administrative reform under General de Gaulle
Jeanneney, Jean-Noël (b. 1942): Head of Radio France and minister under François Mitterrand, 1988–93
Jeanneney, Jules (1864–1967): President of the Senate in 1940
Joliot-Curie, Frédéric (1900–58) and Irène (1897–1956): Nobel laureates in chemistry and supporters of nuclear disarmament
Jospin, Lionel (b. 1937): Leader of the PS 1981–88 and PM 1997–2002
Jouhault, Léon (1879–1954): General Secretary and founder of CGT-FO, 1947
Lagardère, Jean-Luc (b. 1928): Head of publishing-to-armaments conglomerate
Latécoère, Pierre (1883–1943): Commercial aviation pioneer (company created 1919)
Laval, Pierre (1885–1945): PM under Marshal Pétain and chief collaborator with Nazis
Leclerc, André (b. 1903) and Edouard (b. 1926): Founders of supermarket chain of same name, 1963
Lefaucheux, Pierre (1898–1955): CEO of car firm Renault after nationalisation in 1945
Lehideux, François (1905–98): Minister of industrial production in Vichy government, 1941–4
Le Pen, Jean-Marie (b. 1928): Founder and president of extreme right-wing National Front, 1972
Lépine, Louis (1846–1933): Préfet* of Paris and initiator of inventors' competition (*Concours Lépine*)
Leroy-Beaulieu, Paul (1843–1916): Leading free-market economist before the First World War; son-in-law of Michel Chevalier

138 A national portrait gallery of twentieth-century France

Loucheur, Louis (1872–1931): Supervisor of industrial mobilisation in the Second World War; initiator of popular subsidised housing, 1928

Lumière, Auguste (1862–1954) and Louis (1864–1948): Pioneers of filmmaking and commercial cinema

Lyautey, Hubert (1862–1954): Pacifier and coloniser of Morocco

Madelin, Alain (b. 1946): Thatcherite industry minister in 1986–8 and short-lived finance minister, 1995

Maire, Edmond (b. 1931): Long-serving general secretary of CFDT union, 1971–89

Mandel, Georges (1885–1944): Clemenceau's chief of staff and leading Radical minister

Mauriac, François (1885–1970): Nobel prize for literature 1952

Mauroy, Pierre (b. 1924) long-serving Socialist Mayor of Lille; PM 1981–4

Maurras, Charles (1868–1952): Monarchist leader and Provençal revivalist; greeted 1940 invasion as 'a divine surprise'

Méline, Jules (1838–1925): Farm minister in the First World War and advocate of farming protectionism

Mendès France, Pierre (1907–82): Radical PM in 1954–5; signed peace treaty with Indochina, 1954

Messier, Jean-Marie (b. 1956): Controversial founder and head of Vivendi Universal

Michelin, François (b. 1926): CEO of famous tyres, road maps and guide books family empire

Mitterrand, François (1916–1996): Minister under the Fourth Republic; fourth President of the Fifth Republic, 1981–95

Mollet, Guy (1905–75): Socialist leader and PM 1956–7; responsible for failed Suez expedition in 1956

Monnet, Jean (1888–1979): Initiator of industrial planning; advocate of European integration

Moreau, Emile (1877–1959): Governor of the Banque de France,* 1926–30

Moulin, Jean (1899–1943): Co-ordinator of the French resistance; first president of the CNR

Pétain, Philippe (1856–1952): 'Hero of Verdun'; head of the French (Vichy) state 1940–4

Peugeot, François (1900–85): CEO of car-maker Peugeot, until 1975 a family firm

Piaf, Edith (Giovanna Gassion, 1915–63): Popular singer in the 1930s and 1940s

Pierre, Abbé (Henri Groués, b. 1912): Founder of Emmaüs, a charity for the homeless

Pinault, François (b. 1936): CEO of the Printemps-Redoute distribution group

Pinay, Antoine (1891–1994): PM 1952 and stabiliser of the franc (Pinay bonds)
Pisani, Edgard (b. 1918): Farm minister 1961–6; promoter of farm support scheme (FORMA)
Pleven, René (1901–93): Finance minister in 1945; defence minister 1952–4; promoter of CED/FDC
Poincaré, Raymond (1860–1934): President of the Republic 1913–20; 'saviour of the franc' as PM 1926–8
Pompidou, Georges (1911–74): Second President of the Fifth Republic, 1969–74
Poujade, Pierre (b. 1920): Shopkeeper and craftsman activist; founded the UDCA in 1953
Pucheu, Pierre (1899–1944): Vichy interior minister and police chief
Queuille, Henri (1884–1970): Agriculture minister 1924–40; Radical PM 1948–9 and 1950
Renault, Louis (1877–1944): CEO and founder of the Renault car firm
Reynaud, Paul (1878–1966): PM 1940
Ribot, Alexandre (1842–1923): Finance minister during the First World War
Riboud, Antoine (1918–2002): CEO and founder of BSN-Gervais-Danone, a food conglomerate
Rocard, Michel (b. 1930): Socialist PM 1988–91
de Rothschild, Edmond (1926–97): CEO of Banque Rothschild
Rueff, Jacques (1896–1978): Director of the Treasury and promoter of the 'new' franc, 1959
de Saint-Exupéry, Antoine (1900–44): Second World War pilot and popular author
Saint-Laurent, Yves (b. 1936): Founder of haute couture firm of same name
Sangnier, Marc (1874–1950): Editor of *Le Sillon* and inspirer of Christian Democracy
Sarrault, Albert (1872–1962): Transition PM in 1933 and 1936
Saunier-Séïté, Alice (1925–2003): Minister for the universities 1976–8; family minister 1984–86
Sauvy, Alfred (1898–1990): Leading economist and demographer
Schuman, Robert (1886–1963): PM 1948; foreign minister 1948–53
Schweitzer, Louis (b. 1942): CEO of Renault since 1992 (privatised 1997)
Séguy, Georges (b. 1927): General secretary of the CGT Union 1967–82
Sellières, Ernest-Antoine (b. 1937): President of CNPF since 1997 (became MEDEF in 1998)
Servan-Schreiber, Jean-Jacques (b. 1924): Influential editor of *L'Express* magazine
Simiand, François (1873–1935): France's leading economist and price theorist

Taittinger, Pierre (1887–1965): Champagne magnate and founder of the Jeunesses Patriotes, a right-wing league, 1924

Tardieu, André (1876–1945): Right-leaning PM 1929–30; initiator of industrial planning

Thomas, Albert (1878–1932): Armaments minister, 1917; President of ILO 1920–32

Thorez, Maurice (1900–64): Communist leader and cabinet minister 1945–7

Tillon, Charles (1897–1993): Communist armaments minister, 1946–7

Trichet, Jean-Claude (b. 1942): Governor of the Banque de France* since 1993, and of the ECB as of 1 November 2003

Trigano, Gilbert (1920–2001): Founder of Club Méditerranée, 1950

Veil, Simone (b. 1927): Health minister under Valéry Giscard d'Estaing; President of the European Parliament 1979–82

Weiss, Louise (1893–1983): Feminist activist in the interwar years and European federalist

de Wendel, François (1874–1949): Steel industrialist; president of the Comité des Forges

Zay, Jean (1904–44): Education minister of the Popular Front 1936–7

Bibliography

Adams, William J. (1989). *Restructuring the French Economy. Government and the Rise of Market Competition since World War II*. Washington: The Brookings Institution.
Adams, William J. & Christian Stoffaës (1986), eds. *French Industrial Policy*. Washington: The Brookings Institution.
Albert, Michel (1991). *Capitalisme contre capitalisme*. Paris: Le Seuil.
Allaire, G. & R. Boyer (1995). *La grande transformation de l'agriculture*. Paris: INRA.
Andrews, William G. & Stanley Hoffmann, eds. *The Fifth Republic at Twenty*. Albany: State University of New York Press.
Andrieu, Claire (1984). *Le programme commun de la Résistance. Des idées dans la guerre*. Paris: Editions de l'Erudit.
Asselain, Jean-Charles (1984). *Histoire économique de la Frnace du XVIIIe siècle à nos jours*. Paris: Le Seuil.
Asselain, Jean-Charles & Christian Morrisson (1983). 'Economic growth and interest groups: the French experience', in Dennis C. Mueller, ed., *The Political Economy of Growth*. New Haven: Yale University Press, pp. 157–75.
Auquier, Antoine (1984). *French Industry's Reaction to the European Common Market*. New York: Garland.
Barjot, Dominique (1995). *Histoire économique de la France au XIXe siècle*. Paris: Nathan.
Baum, Warren C. (1958). *The French Economy and the State*. Princeton: Princeton University Press.
Baverez, Nicolas (1998). *Les trente piteuses*. Paris: Le Seuil.
Beltran, Alain & Pascal Griset (1994). *La croissance économique en France au XIXe siècle*. Paris: Armand Colin.
Bloch-Lainé, François & Jean-Bouvier (1986). *La France Restaurée, 1944–1954. Dialogue sur les choix d'une modernisation*. Paris: Fayard.
Boltho, Andrea (1982), ed. *The European Economy: Growth and Crisis*. New York: Oxford University Press.

Bourdieu, Pierre (1977). *Reproduction in Education, Society and Culture.* London: Sage.

Brender, Anton (1998). *La France face à la mondialisation,* Paris: La Découverte.

Caron, François (1979). *An Economic History of Modern France.* London: Methuen.

Carré, Jean-Jacques, Paul Dubois & Edmond Malinvaud (1975). *French Economic Growth.* Stanford University Press.

Charvet, Jean-Pierre (1994). *La France agricole en état de choc.* Paris: Liris.

Clough, Shepard B. (1939). *France: A History of National Economics, 1789–1939.* New York: Scribner's.

Cohen, Elie (1995). 'France: national champions in search of a mission' in Jack Hayward, ed., *Industrial Enterprise and European Integration.* Oxford: Oxford University Press, pp. 245–72.

Cohen, Elie (1996). *La tentation hexagonale: la souveraineté à l'épreuve de la mondialisation.* Paris: Fayard.

Cotta, Alain (1995). *La troisième révolution française.* Paris: Jean-Claude Lattès.

Crozier, Michel (1960). *Le phénomène bureaucratique.* Paris: Presses Universitaires de France.

Delorme, Robert & Christine André (1981). *L'Etat et l'économie. Essai d'explication de l'évolution des dépenses publiques en France.* Paris: Le Seuil.

Dessirier, Jean (1935). 'Secteurs "abrités" et "non-abrités" dans le déséquilibre actuel de l'économie française,' *Revue d'Economie Politique* 49: 1330–58.

Dobbin, Frank (1990). *Forging Industrial Policy. The United States, Britain and France in the Railway Age.* Cambridge: Cambridge University Press.

Dormois, Jean-Pierre (1997). *L'économie française face à la concurrence britannique avant 1914.* Paris: L'Harmattan.

Dormois, Jean-Pierre (1998a). 'France: the idiosyncrasies of interventionism', in J. Foreman-Peck & G. Federico, eds., *A Century of European Industrial Policy.* Oxford: Oxford University Press, pp. 58–97.

Dormois, Jean-Pierre (1998b). 'The significance of the French colonial empire for French economic development (1815–1960)', *Revista de Historia Económica* 16: 323–49.

Dormois, Jean-Pierre (2004). 'Episodes in catching-up. Anglo-French productivity in industry in 1930', *European Review of Economic History* (forthcoming).

Eck, Jean-François (1994). *La France dans la nouvelle économie mondiale.* Paris: Presses Universitaires de France.

Estrin, Saul & Peter Holmes (1983). *French Planning in Theory and Practice.* London: Allen & Unwin.

Fontaine, Arthur (1926). *French Industry during the War.* New Haven: Yale University Press.

Fourastié, Jean (1979). *Les Trente Glorieuses ou la Révolution invisible de 1946 à 1975.* Paris: Fayard.

Garrigues, Jean (2002), ed. *Les groupes de pression dans la vie politique contemporaine en France et aux Etats-Unis de 1820 à nos jours.* Rennes: Presses Universitaires.

Gauchon, Pascal (2002). *Le modèle français.* Paris: Presses Universitaires de France.

Goreux, Louis-Marie (1977). *Agricultural Productivity and Economic Development in France 1852–1950.* New York: Arno Press.

Gravier, Jean-François (1947). *Paris et le désert français.* Paris: Presses Universitaires de France.

Gueslin, André (1994). *Nouvelle histoire économique de la France contemporaine,* vol. 4, *L'économie ouverte 1948–90.* Paris: La Découverte.

Hall, Peter A. (1986). *Governing the Economy. The Politics of State Intervention in Britain and France.* New York: Oxford University Press.

Hayward, Jack & Michael Watson (1985), eds. *The State and the Market Economy: Industrial Patriotism and Economic Intervention in France.* Brighton: Wheatsheaf.

Jeanneney, Jean-Marcel (1959). *Forces et faiblesses de l'économie française.* Paris: Armand Colin.

Kaelble, Hartmut (2003), ed. *The European Way. The Societies of Europe in the Nineteenth and Twentieth Centuries.* Oxford: Berghahn.

Kemp, Tom (1972). *The French Economy 1919–1939. The History of a Decline.* London: Frank Cass.

Kindleberger, Charles (1964). *Economic Growth in Britain and France 1851–1950.* Cambridge, MA: Harvard University Press.

Kuisel, Robert (1981). *Capitalism and the State in Modern France. Renovation and Economic Management in the Twentieth Century.* Cambridge: Cambridge University Press.

Landes, David (1951). 'French business and the businessman: a social and cultural analysis' in Edward M. Earle, ed., *Problems of the Third and Fourth Republics.* Princeton: Princeton University Press.

Lauffenberger, Henri (1939). *L'intervention de l'Etat en matière économique.* Paris: Presses Universitaires de France.

Levet, Jean-Louis (1985). *Les dossiers noirs de l'industrie française: échecs, handicaps, espoirs.* Paris: Fayard.

Lévy-Leboyer, Maurice (1996), ed. *Histoire de la France industrielle.* Paris: Larousse.

Lévy-Leboyer, Maurice & Jean-Claude Casanova (1991), eds. *Entre l'Etat et le marché.* Paris: Gallimard.

Limouzin, Pierre (1995). *L'agriculture et les industries agroalimentaires françaises.* Paris: Masson.

Bibliography

Lynch, Frances (1997). *A History of the French Economy: From Vichy to Rome 1944–1958*. London: Routledge.

McArthur, John H. & Bruce R. Scott (1969). *Industrial Planning in France*. Boston: Harvard University Business School.

Maddison, Angus (1995). *Monitoring the World Economy 1820–1992*. Paris: OECD.

Maddison, Angus (2001). *The World Economy: A Millennium Perspective*. Paris: OECD.

Marchand, Olivier & Claude Thélot (1991). *Deux siècles de travail en France*. Paris: Nathan.

Marco, Luc (1989). *La montée des faillites en France (XIXe–XXe siècle)*. Paris: L'Harmattan.

Margairaz, Michel (1991). *L'Etat, les Finances et l'économie. Histoire d'une conversion 1932–1952*. Paris: Imprimerie Nationale.

Marseille, Jacques (1984). *Empire colonial et capitalisme français*. Paris: Albin Michel.

Mendras, Henri (1967). *La fin des paysans*. Paris: Presses Universitaires de France.

Milward, Alan (1970). *The New Order and the French Economy*. Oxford: Clarendon Press.

Ogburn, William & Jerome Jaffé (1929). *The Economic Development of Postwar France. A Survey of Production*. New York: Columbia University Press.

Olson, Mancur (1982). *The Rise and Decline of Nations. Economic Growth, Stagflation and Social Rigidities*. New Haven: Yale University Press.

Petit-Dutaillis, G. (1974). *La banque française: évolution des activités et des structures*. Paris/New York: McGraw-Hill.

Piketti, Thomas (2001). *Les hauts revenus en France au XX siècle*. Paris: Grasset.

Polanyi, Karl (1944). *The Great Transformation*. Boston: Beacon Press.

Rosanvallon, Pierre (1990). *L'Etat en France de 1789 à nos jours*. Paris: Le Seuil.

Rosenberg, Nathan & L. E. Birdzell, Jr. (1984). *How the West Grew Rich. The Economic Transformation of the Industrial World*. New York: Basic Books.

Salais, R., N. Baverez & B. Reynaud (1986). *L'invention du chômage*. Paris: Presses Universitaires de France.

Saly, Pierre (1980). *La politique des Grands Travaux en France 1929–1939*. New York: Arno Press.

Sartre, Jean-Paul (1946). *L'existentialisme est un humanisme*. Paris: Nagel.

Schuker, Stephen A. (1976). *The End of French Predominance in Europe. The Financial Crisis of 1924 and the Adoption of the Dawes Plan*. Chapel Hill: University of North Carolina Press.

Bibliography 145

Sheanan, John (1963). *Promotion and Control of Industry in Postwar France*. Cambridge, MA: Harvard University Press.

Sicsic, Pierre & Charles Wyplosz (1996). 'France, 1945–1992', in Nicholas Crafts and Gianni Toniolo, eds., *Economic Growth in Europe Since 1945*. Cambridge: Cambridge University Press, pp. 210–39.

Suleiman, Ezra N. (1993). *France: the Transformation of a Society*. Princeton: Princeton University Press.

Taddéi, Dominique & Benjamin Coriat (1993). *Made in France. L'industrie française dans la compétition mondiale*. Paris: Librairie Générale de France.

Tilly, Charles (1986). *The Contentious French*. Cambridge, MA: Harvard University Press.

Toutain, Jean-Claude (1997). 'La croissance française 1789–1990. Nouvelles estimations', *Economies et Sociétés* Série HEQ no. 11 (November).

Vesperini, Jean-Pierre (2001), ed. *Les problèmes actuels de l'économie française*. Paris: Presses Universitaires de France.

Index

Acte Unique 68
Aérospatiale 74
affluent society 18
Africa 36, 83
agriculture 101, 102, 103, 107
Air France 56, 85, 124
Alcatel 74
Algeria 36, 130
Americanisation 1, 7
anti-capitalism, anti-capitalist 87, 95
anti-globalisation 63
anti-trust (legislation) 68
Armand, Louis 69, 80
Auchan 125
automatic stabilisers 22, 24, 59
AXA 125

baby boom 3, 46, 83, 88, 96
balance of payments 24, 34, 35, 38, 40, 43, 56
balance of trade 55, 124
balanced growth 102, 103
banks, banking 59, 68, 69, 123
bankruptcy 66, 67
Banque de France 16, 53, 69, 125
Banque Populaire 53
bargaining power 91
Beauce 108
Belle Epoque 12, 17
beurs 5
birth rate 2, 3
black market 17, 106
bonds 16, 66, 68, 123
boom 24
Bourdieu, Pierre 81

Bové, José 63, 109
Bretton Woods 22, 39
Brie 108
Brittany 124
budget 16, 23
budget deficit 48
bureaucracy 130
Burgundy 108
business creation, start-up 64, 65, 76
business cycle 18, 99
business history 128
business schools 74

cadres 99, 117
Cameron, Rondo 113
CAP 101, 108, 109, 110, 111, 130
capital flight 16, 54
capital formation 23, 116
capital intensity 114
capital markets 117
capitalism 58, 63, 79, 115, 130
captive markets 119
Carrefour 124, 125
cartels 67, 119
Casino 124
catching up 18
CGP 58, 115
chain stores 123
Charter of Amiens 77, 78
cheque 68
cités 130
Clemenceau, Georges 47, 66
Clémentel, Etienne 79
'closed shop' 79
Club Med 125
CNR 58, 115

146

Index 147

CNRS 74
COB 69
Code Civil 2
Code de commerce 65
Code de la Famille 61
Colbert, J. B. 43
collective bargaining 21, 52
colonisation 36
Combes, Emile 71
comité d'entreprise 21
commercial law 67
Common Market 108
communications 57
Communist(s) 58, 78
comparative advantage 32, 33, 41, 70
competition 28, 51, 64, 69, 122, 126, 127, 131
concentration 67, 68, 86
Congress of Berlin 36
Conseil d'Etat 51
consortiums 33
consumer goods 14, 114, 119
consumer society 11
consumption 21, 119
controls, wartime 51
convertibility 16, 39, 55
convergence 1
corporate law 66
corporate services 120
Corporation paysanne 106
corporatism, corporatist 51, 63–4, 76, 77, 104, 115
corps intermédiaires 77
costs, production 110
credit 117
Crédit Agricole 53
Crédit National 53
cross-financing 117, 126
Crozier, Michel 81
customs duties 34

death rate 3
Debré, Michel 57
debt 53
decolonization 119
deflation 48
de-industrialisation 92, 99, 112
Delors, Jacques 24
demand 119
demand management 52, 59
demography 1, 2, 5, 36

depression of the 1930s 58, 77, 85, 97, 104
deregulation 26, 69, 112
désert français 10
devaluation 19, 59
dirigisme 43, 57, 112
division of labour 27
domestic service 123
Dorgelès, Roland 104
double occupation 96
Dreyfus affair 71
droits acquis 79, 91
dualism, dual economy 77
Duteurtre, Benoît 9

earnings 125
economies of scale 86, 117, 123
education 70, 71, 73–4, 95, 99
egalitarianism 129
electoral system 102
employers 79
employment 8, 43, 46, 47, 51, 61, 64, 86, 88, 89, 91, 92, 93, 115, 119, 120, 125
Engel's law 87
entrepreneurs, entrepreneurship 64, 65, 113
Ericsson 57
EU 101
European integration 24, 27, 40, 56, 59, 64, 129
exception française 1
exchange controls 55, 69
existentialism 10
expatriates 129

family firm 65, 121, 123
farm exports 108, 109
farm imports 103
farm, farming 14, 83, 101, 102, 103, 107, 108, 110, 111, 130
farming, traditional 102, 103
Faure, Edgar 73
Ferry, Jules 71
fertility rate 3, 4, 6, 88
fertilisers 106, 107
financial services 123, 126
'fine tuning' 59
FME 59
fonction publique 45
food processing 111

foodstuffs 101, 106, 109, 111
Ford, Henry 117
Fourastié, Jean 6
franc 54, 69
franc zone 19, 40

GATT 28, 39
Gaulle, Charles de 66, 67, 78, 115, 128
GEN 117
Gide, Charles 96
globalisation 23, 27, 28, 31
GNP/GDP 16, 21, 23, 24, 31, 54, 57, 62, 74, 112, 125
Gold standard 34
Golden Age 12, 17, 57, 60, 67, 68, 71, 78, 82, 85, 86, 91, 97, 109, 117
government 1, 19, 40, 43, 44, 45, 46, 47, 48, 51, 52, 56, 57, 58, 59, 61, 68, 69, 71, 73, 79, 116, 123, 129
government control 73–4
government employment 44
government intervention 52, 69, 112
government revenue 48, 64
grandes écoles 73, 74
grands corps 80
'green shirts' 104
Great Depression 4, 13, 96
great transformation 50
growth 13, 15
guilds 123

Haby, René 73
Hanau, Marthe 66
Havas 125
health insurance 61
hexagon 128
'high farming' 106
human capital 70, 73, 93, 116

illiteracy (economic) 131
immigrants 2, 4, 5, 60, 96, 125
imperialism 36, 37
imports 104
import quotas 104
income(s) 11, 17, 21, 93, 103, 108, 110
income tax 16, 47, 48
incorporation 66, 76
industrial actions 52
industrial policy 116

industrial production 113, 114, 115
industrial relations 52
industrial revolution, industrialisation 13, 14, 27, 85, 102
industrialists 87
industry 55, 56, 112, 116, 119, 124, 125
inflation 19, 26, 34, 35, 53, 68, 69
information 95
infrastructures 115, 130
innovation, technological 64, 65, 74, 76
INRA 107
INSEE 59
insurance 125
interest groups 29
interest rates 24, 69
international position 27, 120
interventionism 50, 52, 56, 58
inventions 75
investment 19, 24, 26, 31, 32, 37, 39, 42, 53, 69, 107, 113, 117

job market 96, 100
joint stock 67

Keynes, J. M. 58

labour income 93
labour market 26, 52, 82, 89, 97, 100, 120
labour organisations, movement 78, 79
laissez-faire 50, 65
Laval, Pierre 67
Leclerc, Edouard 124
leisure 82, 129
Lenin, V. I. 78
Leroy-Beaulieu, Paul 50
life expectancy 3, 8, 61
lifestyles 85
limited liability 66, 67
literacy 71
living conditions 102
living standards 11, 15, 21, 50, 125
Lorraine 10, 77
Louis XIV 43

machinery 87, 106
macroeconomic policy 59
Malthusianism 2, 113

Index   149

management, managers 117
manufacturing 113, 124, 126
Margairaz, Michel 116
market forces, mechanisms 44, 63–4, 126, 130, 131
marketing boards 104, 107
Marseille(s) 86
Marshall Plan/Aid 17, 57, 59, 75, 107, 116
May 1968 87, 131
Mediterranean 129, 130
Meissier, Jean-Marie 1, 124
Méline tariff 29, 33
Mendras, Henri 101
mercantilism 43
mergers 13, 67, 69, 87, 115
mezzogiorno 130
middle class 14
migrations 13, 36, 85, 110, 123
minette 113
minimum wage 52, 62, 92
Mitterrand, François 62, 64, 81
mixed banking 68
mixed company 56
modernisation 128
monetary policy 55
Monnet, Jean 58, 65, 115
monopoly 79, 80
Monoprix 123
mortality rate 3
motive power 114
multinationals 75

national champions 43, 67
national income 35
nationalisation 53, 69, 120
Nazi Germany 106
New Deal 58
Nobel prize 75
nomenklatura 80
Nord 10
Normandy 125
nuclear family 4

O'Brien, Patrick K. 122
OECD 87
Offer, Avner 121
oil shock 19, 22, 23, 26, 39, 40, 48, 58, 59, 92, 97, 119, 124
ONIB 57
openness 27, 28, 31, 35, 40

Orwell, George 64
output, industrial 86

'*pantouflage*' 80
Pareto, Vilfredo 81
Paris 11
paritarisme 52, 78, 92
participation rates 26, 83, 88, 97
Pasteur, Louis 122
patents 75
pensions 61, 62, 79, 80, 130
personal services 121, 122
Picardy 108
pieds noirs 5
Pigier 74
Pisani, Edgard 108
planning, plans 58, 59
'ploughing back' 117
Poincaré, Raymond
Polanyi, Karl 64
Pompidou, Georges 33, 86
Popular Front 53, 104
population 1, 2, 3, 85, 97, 120, 123
postal service 124, 125
postindustrial 87
preferences 121
price(s) 103, 107, 109, 110, 123
price fixing 107
private sector 120
privatisation 79
procurement 40, 74, 119
production 15, 17, 18
production, flexible 87
production, mass 87, 95
productivity 18, 19, 85, 95, 103, 113, 122, 126
professions (learned) 123, 126
profits, profitability 16, 37, 47, 69, 122, 125
protectionism 33, 55
prudential goods 121
public employment 45, 46
public revenue 48
public (state) sector 45, 46, 47, 52, 56, 130
public service(s) 46, 56, 79, 80, 129
public spending or expenditure 48, 50
public utilities 117
public works 56
Publicis 125

Index

pump priming 24, 59, 116
putting-out 114

Quesnay, François 101
quotas 34, 39, 119

Radicals 71
R&D 74, 75
ratchet mechanism 46
rationing 17, 34, 106
Reconstruction 15, 17, 18, 19, 22, 34, 56, 67, 88
redistribution 126
regulation 57
rentiers 16
republican 43, 44
restrictions, restritive practices 29, 52
retail trade 123, 124
retardation 65, 113
retirement 8, 52, 62, 79
Ripert, Georges 66
RMI 62
Romain, Jules 122
Rueff, Jacques 69, 80

salary 7
Sauvy, Alfred 113
saving rate, savings 68
Say, Léon 81
school(s), schooling 70, 71, 73, 74, 95
school-leaving age 71
secondary sector 112
securities 117
self-sufficiency 14, 43
semi-finished goods 114
services 87, 88, 89, 91, 120, 121, 122, 123, 124, 125
sex discrimination 89
Sieburg, Friedrich 6, 9, 82, 131
SNCF 56, 124
social contributions 62
social insurance 61
social market (economy) 129
social security 38, 48, 50, 61, 119
social services 60
social transfers 61
Socialism, Socialist(s) 47, 56, 58, 64, 69, 71, 78, 81
Sombart, Wilhelm 63
specialisation 41
stagflation 23, 59
stagnation 2, 83, 113
standard of living 103, 121
staple foods 108, 109, 110
state, as 'nightwatchman' 50
status quo 113
stock market 37, 117, 123
'stop-and-go' 59
stress 93
strikes 77
students 8
subsidies 56, 69, 71, 104, 108
subsistence farming 103
Sully, Duke of 101
supermarkets 51, 80, 124
surplus(es) 108, 109

takeovers 13
tariffs 32, 104, 107
tastes 104
Tati, Jacques 6, 85, 106
taxation 16, 48, 57
Taylor, Frederick W. 117
technocrats, technocracy 80
technology 15, 86
telecoms 124, 125
telephone service 57
tertiary (service) sector 88, 120, 121, 122, 124
Thomson, C. S. F. 74
Thorez, Maurice 115
Tocqueville, Alexis de 128
tourism 125, 130
trade 19, 23, 32, 34, 38, 39, 55
trade barriers 104
trade deficit 107
trade unions 77, 78, 79, 92, 109
training 70, 71, 73, 93, 95, 99
transfers, technology 75
transport 123
Treasury 52, 53, 58, 59, 69, 117
Trente Glorieuses 6, 11, 17
Trigano, Gilbert 125

underemployment 97
unemployment 8, 24, 26, 60, 61, 82, 83, 88, 89, 91, 92, 93, 95, 96, 97, 99, 100, 129

Index   151

unionization 77
universal suffrage 88
university 73
upward mobility 81
urban, urbanisation 10, 14, 85, 102
utopia 102

value added 119
VAT 48
Vichy 58, 116
Vivendi 1, 124

wages 91
Wagner, Adolf 46
way of life (French) 9
wealth, national 54
wealth tax 48

welfare, welfare state, system 21, 50, 60, 62, 64, 126, 131
Wendel 68, 119
wine 103, 104, 108
women 88, 89, 102
work contracts 92
work ethic 95, 131
workers, foreign 83
workers, industrial 60, 117, 119
workforce, working population 7, 16, 26, 46, 62, 82, 83, 97, 99, 102, 113, 114, 117, 124, 125, 129
working attitudes 95
working conditions 52, 89
working time 7, 9, 89, 91
works councils 52

yields 103–4, 107

Previously published as

New Studies in Economic and Social History

Titles in the series available from Cambridge University Press:

1. M. Anderson *Approaches to the history of the Western family, 1500–1914*
   ISBN 0 521 55260 5 (hardback) 0 521 55793 3 (paperback)
2. W. Macpherson *The economic development of Japan, 1868–1941*
   ISBN 0 521 55792 5 (hardback) 0 521 55261 3 (paperback)
3. R. Porter *Disease, medicine, and society in England: second edition*
   ISBN 0 521 55262 1 (hardback) 0 521 55791 7 (paperback)
4. B. W. E. Alford *British economic performance since 1945*
   ISBN 0 521 55263 X (hardback) 0 521 55790 9 (paperback)
5. A. Crowther *Social policy in Britain, 1914–1939*
   ISBN 0 521 55264 8 (hardback) 0 521 55789 5 (paperback)
6. E. Roberts *Women's work 1840–1940*
   ISBN 0 521 55265 6 (hardback) 0 521 55788 7 (paperback)
7. C. O'Gráda *The great Irish famine*
   ISBN 0 521 55266 4 (hardback) 0 521 55787 9 (paperback)
8. R. Rodger *Housing in urban Britain 1780–1914*
   ISBN 0 521 55267 2 (hardback) 0 521 55786 0 (paperback)
9. P. Slack *The English poor law 1531–1782*
   ISBN 0 521 55268 0 (hardback) 0 521 55785 2 (paperback)
10. J. L. Anderson *Explaining long-term economic change*
    ISBN 0 521 55269 9 (hardback) 0 521 55784 4 (paperback)
11. D. Baines *Emigration from Europe 1815–1930*
    ISBN 0 521 55270 2 (hardback) 0 521 55783 6 (paperback)
12. M. Collins *Banks and industrial finance 1800–1939*
    ISBN 0 521 55271 0 (hardback) 0 521 55782 8 (paperback)
13. A. Dyer *Decline and growth in English towns 1400–1640*
    ISBN 0 521 55272 9 (hardback) 0 521 55781 X (paperback)

14. R. B. Outhwaite *Dearth, public policy and social disturbance in England, 1550–1800*
    ISBN 0 521 55273 7 (hardback) 0 521 55780 1 (paperback)
15. M. Sanderson *Education, economic change and society in England*
    ISBN 0 521 55274 5 (hardback) 0 521 55779 8 (paperback)
16. R. D. Anderson *Universities and elites in Britain since 1800*
    ISBN 0 521 55275 3 (hardback) 0 521 55778 X (paperback)
17. C. Heywood *The development of the French economy, 1700–1914*
    ISBN 0 521 55276 1 (hardback) 0 521 55777 1 (paperback)
18. R. A. Houston *The population history of Britain and Ireland 1500–1750*
    ISBN 0 521 55277 X (hardback) 0 521 55776 3 (paperback)
19. A. J. Reid *Social classes and social relations in Britain 1850–1914*
    ISBN 0 521 55278 8 (hardback) 0 521 55775 5 (paperback)
20. R. Woods *The population of Britain in the nineteenth century*
    ISBN 0 521 55279 6 (hardback) 0 521 55774 7 (paperback)
21. T. C. Barker *The rise and rise of road transport, 1700–1990*
    ISBN 0 521 55280 X (hardback) 0 521 55773 9 (paperback)
22. J. Harrison *The Spanish economy*
    ISBN 0 521 55281 8 (hardback) 0 521 55772 0 (paperback)
23. C. Schmitz *The growth of big business in the United States and Western Europe, 1850–1939*
    ISBN 0 521 55282 6 (hardback) 0 521 55771 2 (paperback)
24. R. A. Church *The rise and decline of the British motor industry*
    ISBN 0 521 55283 4 (hardback) 0 521 55770 4 (paperback)
25. P. Horn *Children's work and welfare, 1780–1880*
    ISBN 0 521 55284 2 (hardback) 0 521 55769 0 (paperback)
26. R. Perren *Agriculture in depression, 1870–1940*
    ISBN 0 521 55285 0 (hardback) 0 521 55768 2 (paperback)
27. R. J. Overy *The Nazi economic recovery 1932–1938: second edition*
    ISBN 0 521 55286 9 (hardback) 0 521 55767 4 (paperback)
28. S. Cherry *Medical services and the hospitals in Britain, 1860–1939*
    ISBN 0 521 57126 X (hardback) 0 521 57784 5 (paperback)
29. D. Edgerton *Science, technology and the British industrial 'decline', 1870–1970*
    ISBN 0 521 57127 8 (hardback) 0 521 57778 0 (paperback)
30. C. A. Whatley *The Industrial Revolution in Scotland*
    ISBN 0 521 57228 2 (hardback) 0 521 57643 1 (paperback)

31. H. E. Meller *Towns, plans and society in modern Britain*
    ISBN 0 521 57227 4 (hardback) 0 521 57644 X (paperback)
32. H. Hendrick *Children, childhood and English society, 1880–1990*
    ISBN 0 521 57253 3 (hardback) 0 521 57624 5 (paperback)
33. N. Tranter *Sport, economy and society in Britain, 1750–1914*
    ISBN 0 521 57217 7 (hardback) 0 521 57655 5 (paperback)
34. R. W. Davies *Soviet economic development from Lenin to Khrushchev*
    ISBN 0 521 62260 3 (hardback) 0 521 62742 7 (paperback)
35. H. V. Bowen *War and British society, 1688–1815*
    ISBN 0 521 57226 6 (hardback) 0 521 57645 8 (paperback)
36. M. M. Smith *Debating slavery: the antebellum American south*
    ISBN 0 521 57158 8 (hardback) 0 521 57696 2 (paperback)
37. M. Sanderson *Education and economic decline in Britain, 1870 to the 1990s*
    ISBN 0 521 58170 2 (hardback) 0 521 58842 1 (paperback)
38. V. Berridge *Health policy, health and society, 1939 to the 1990s*
    ISBN 0 521 57230 4 (hardback) 0 521 57641 5 (paperback)
39. M. E. Mate *Women in medieval English society*
    ISBN 0 521 58322 5 (hardback) 0 521 58733 6 (paperback)
40. P. J. Richardson *Economic change in China c. 1800–1950*
    ISBN 0 521 58396 9 (hardback) 0 521 63571 3 (paperback)
41. J. E. Archer *Social unrest and popular protest in England, 1780–1840*
    ISBN 0 521 57216 9 (hardback) 0 521 57656 3 (paperback)
42. K. Morgan *Slavery, Atlantic trade and the British economy, 1660–1800*
    ISBN 0 521 58213 X (hardback) 0 521 58814 6 (paperback)
43. C. W. Chalklin *The rise of the English town, 1650–1850*
    ISBN 0 521 66141 2 (hardback) 0 521 66737 2 (paperback)
44. J. Cohen and G. Federico *The growth of the Italian economy, 1820–1960*
    ISBN 0 521 66150 1 (hardback) 0 521 66692 9 (paperback)
45. T. Balderston *Economics and politics in the Weimar Republic*
    ISBN 0 521 58375 6 (hardback) 0 521 77760 7 (paperback)
46. C. Wrigley *British Trade Unions since 1933*
    ISBN 0 521 57231 2 (hardback) 0 521 57640 7 (paperback)
47. A. Colli *The History of Family Business, 1850–2000*
    ISBN 0 521 80028 5 (hardback) 0 521 80472 8 (paperback)
48. D. Mühlberger *The Social Bases of Nazism, 1919–1933*
    ISBN 0 521 80285 7 (hardback) 0 521 00372 5 (paperback)
49. J. P. Dormois *The French Economy in the Twentieth Century*
    ISBN 0 521 66092 0 (hardback) 0 521 66787 9 (paperback)

Titles in the series available from the Macmillan Press Limited

1. B. W. E. Alford *Depression and recovery? British economic growth, 1918–1939*
2. M. Anderson *Population change in north-western Europe, 1750–1850*
3. S. D. Chapman *The cotton industry in the industrial revolution: second edition*
4. M. E. Falkus *The industrialisation of Russia, 1700–1914*
5. J. R. Harris *The British iron industry, 1700–1850*
6. J. Hatcher *Plague, population and the English economy, 1348–1530*
7. J. R. Hay *The origins of the Liberal welfare reforms, 1906–1914*
8. H. McLeod *Religion and the working classes in nineteenth-century Britain*
9. J. D. Marshall *The Old Poor Law 1795–1834: second edition*
10. R. J. Morris *Class and class consciousness in the industrial revolution, 1750–1850*
11. P. K. O'Brien *The economic effects of the American civil war*
12. S. B. Paul *The myth of the Great Depression, 1873–1896: second edition*
13. P. L. Payne *British entrepreneurship in the nineteenth century*
14. G. C. Peden *Keynes, the treasury and British economic policy*
15. M. E. Rose *The relief of poverty, 1834–1914*
16. J. Thirsk *England's agricultural regions and agrarian history, 1500–1750*
17. J. R. Ward *Poverty and progress in the Caribbean, 1800–1960*

Economic History Society

The Economic History Society, which numbers around 3000 members, publishes the *Economic History Review* four times a year (free to members) and holds an annual conference.

Enquiries about membership should be addressed to

> The Assistant Secretary
> Economic History Society
> PO Box 70
> Kingswood
> Bristol
> BS15 5TB

Full-time students may join at special rates.

Printed in Great Britain
by Amazon